A
TREATISE
ON
TOLERATION
AND OTHER
ESSAYS

VOLTAIRE
Translated by Joseph McCabe

GREAT MINDS SERIES

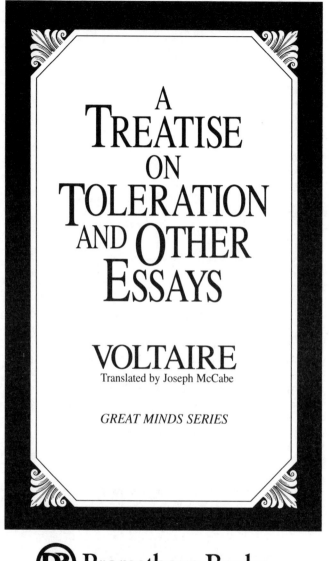 **Prometheus Books**

59 John Glenn Drive
Amherst, New York 14228-2197

Published 1994 by Prometheus Books
59 John Glenn Drive, Amherst, New York 14228-2197.
716-691-0133. FAX: 716-691-0137.

Library of Congress Cataloging-in-Publication Data

Voltaire, 1694–1778.
  [Selections. English. 1994]
  A treatise on toleration and other essays / Voltaire ; translated by Joseph
McCabe.
      p.   cm. — (Great minds series)
  Originally published: Selected works of Voltaire. London : Watts, 1935.
  ISBN 0–87975–881–3 (pbk.)
  1. Christianity—Controversial literature. 2. Bible—Controversial
literature. 3. Religion—Controversial literature. 4. Toleration—Early works
to 1800. I. McCabe, Joseph, 1867–1955. II. Title. III. Series.
B2172.E5   1994
194—dc20   94-3888
                                                                   CIP

Printed in Canada on acid-free paper.

Also Available in Prometheus's Great Minds Paperback Series

Charles Darwin
The Origin of Species

Desiderius Erasmus
The Praise of Folly

Michael Faraday
The Forces of Matter

Galileo Galilei
*Dialogues Concerning
Two New Sciences*

Edward Gibbon
On Christianity

Charlotte Perkins Gilman
Women and Economics

Ernst Haeckel
The Riddle of the Universe

William Harvey
*On the Motion of the Heart and
Blood in Animals*

Herodotus
The History

Julian Huxley
Evolutionary Humanism

Thomas Henry Huxley
*Agnosticism and Christianity
and Other Essays*

Ernest Renan
The Life of Jesus

Adam Smith
Wealth of Nations

Andrew D. White
*A History of the Warfare of
Science with Theology in
Christendom*

See the back of this volume for a complete list of titles in Prometheus's Great Books in Philosophy and Great Minds series.

VOLTAIRE was born François Marie Arouet into a prosperous middle-class family in Paris on November 21, 1694. At the age of ten he was sent to the Jesuit Collège Louis-le-Grand, where he received a thoroughly classical education. After leaving the Collège in 1711, Voltaire began to study law at the prompting of his father, but soon gave this up to devote himself exclusively to writing. In 1715, Voltaire's tragedy *Oedipe* was introduced in Paris. His outspoken lampoons against the aristocracy landed him in the Bastille from 1717 to 1718 (he would again be confined to the Bastille in 1726 for insulting the Chevalier de Rohan); at this time the young Arouet came to be known as Arouet de Voltaire, or simply Voltaire.

From 1726 to 1729, Voltaire, having already achieved considerable fame for his poems and plays and now heir to a comfortable patrimony, resided in England, where he became friends with Queen Caroline (to whom he dedicated his epic poem, *Henriade*) as well as with such literary notables as Alexander Pope. Voltaire praised the freedom of thought and prosperity of England in his *Lettres philosophiques* (otherwise known as *Lettres sur les Anglais*) (1733); this work, along with his *Temple du goût,* an attack on contemporary French literature, resulted in Voltaire's banishment for a while from Paris. He therefore fitted out a retreat, with his companion, Madame du Châtelet, at Cirey, on the borders of Champagne and Lorraine.

Following Madame du Châtelet's death in 1749, Voltaire accepted the offer of Frederick the Great to reside at his court in Potsdam. The relationship soon deteriorated, however; after publishing his libelous pamphlet, *Diatribe du Docteur Akakia,* against Maupertuis, President of the Berlin Academy, Voltaire was arrested but soon released. In 1753, he took to wandering for some years. In 1758, Voltaire purchased a house at Ferney (on the Swiss border, outside Geneva), where he lived with his niece, Madame Denis.

Voltaire's work from this time on became even more outspoken. His poem on the Lisbon earthquake (1755), which opens this volume, is a scathing denunciation of philosophical optimism, which sees all events as willed by God and as the condition of a higher good. This theme would be developed further in what is arguably Voltaire's greatest work, *Candide* (1759).

Voltaire distinguished himself not only as a poet, dramatist, novelist, philosopher, and historian (for his *Siècle de Louis XIV*), but also as a champion of freethought who courageously came to the aid of the victims of religious persecution and fanaticism. While he called himself a theist and espoused a belief in a Prime Mover of the universe, Voltaire rejected special providence, miracles, and divine revelation. He rejected as well personal immortality: human beings are, he says, "machines made like all other animals" and subject to the same immutable laws. Voltaire's creed was a natural religion reducible to a morality whose enlightened goals were justice and an unflinching devotion to truth. Voltaire's famous phrase, *Écrasez l'infâme,* or "Crush the infamous one," would be his war cry against "persecuting and privileged orthodoxy" in general.

Voltaire's house at Ferney became the focal point of many of the most celebrated men of Europe. In 1778, Voltaire, now internationally famous, returned to Paris, after a twenty-five-year absence, for the first performance of his play *Irène*. There he died, in his eighty-fourth year, on May 30, 1778.

Voltaire's other works include *Éléments de la philosophie de Newton* (1738), the philosophical novels *Zadig* (1747) and *Micromégas* (1752), *Essai sur les moeurs* (1756), and *Dictionnaire philosophique* (1764).

Contents

SELECTED WORKS OF

VOLTAIRE

POEM ON THE LISBON DISASTER ;

Or, AN EXAMINATION OF THE AXIOM, "ALL IS WELL"

UNHAPPY mortals ! Dark and mourning earth !
Affrighted gathering of human kind !
Eternal lingering of useless pain !
Come, ye philosophers, who cry, " All's well,"
And contemplate this ruin of a world.
Behold these shreds and cinders of your race,
This child and mother heaped in common wreck,
These scattered limbs beneath the marble shafts—
A hundred thousand whom the earth devours,
Who, torn and bloody, palpitating yet,
Entombed beneath their hospitable roofs,
In racking torment end their stricken lives.
To those expiring murmurs of distress,
To that appalling spectacle of woe,
Will ye reply : " You do but illustrate
The iron laws that chain the will of God " ?
Say ye, o'er that yet quivering mass of flesh :
" God is avenged : the wage of sin is death " ?
What crime, what sin, had those young hearts
    conceived
That lie, bleeding and torn, on mother's breast ?
Did fallen Lisbon deeper drink of vice
Than London, Paris, or sunlit Madrid ?
In these men dance ; at Lisbon yawns the abyss.

Tranquil spectators of your brothers' wreck,
Unmoved by this repellent dance of death,
Who calmly seek the reason of such storms,
Let them but lash your own security;
Your tears will mingle freely with the flood.
When earth its horrid jaws half open shows,
My plaint is innocent, my cries are just.
Surrounded by such cruelties of fate,
By rage of evil and by snares of death,
Fronting the fierceness of the elements,
Sharing our ills, indulge me my lament.
" 'Tis pride," ye say—" the pride of rebel heart,
To think we might fare better than we do."
Go, tell it to the Tagus' stricken banks;
Search in the ruins of that bloody shock;
Ask of the dying in that house of grief,
Whether 'tis pride that calls on heaven for help
And pity for the sufferings of men.
" All's well," ye say, " and all is necessary."
Think ye this universe had been the worse
Without this hellish gulf in Portugal?
Are ye so sure the great eternal cause,
That knows all things, and for itself creates,
Could not have placed us in this dreary clime
Without volcanoes seething 'neath our feet?
Set you this limit to the power supreme?
Would you forbid it use its clemency?
Are not the means of the great artisan
Unlimited for shaping his designs?
The master I would not offend, yet wish
This gulf of fire and sulphur had outpoured
Its baleful flood amid the desert wastes.
God I respect, yet love the universe.
Not pride, alas, it is, but love of man,
To mourn so terrible a stroke as this.

Would it console the sad inhabitants
Of these aflame and desolated shores
To say to them : " Lay down your lives in peace;

For the world's good your homes are sacrificed;
Your ruined palaces shall others build,
For other peoples shall your walls arise;
The North grows rich on your unhappy loss;
Your ills are but a link in general law;
To God you are as those low creeping worms
That wait for you in your predestined tombs " ?
What speech to hold to victims of such ruth !
Add not such cruel outrage to their pain.

Nay, press not on my agitated heart
These iron and irrevocable laws,
This rigid chain of bodies, minds, and worlds.
Dreams of the bloodless thinker are such thoughts.
God holds the chain : is not himself enchained;
By his indulgent choice is all arranged;
Implacable he's not, but free and just.
Why suffer we, then, under one so just? [1]
There is the knot your thinkers should undo.
Think ye to cure our ills denying them?
All peoples, trembling at the hand of God,
Have sought the source of evil in the world.
When the eternal law that all things moves
Doth hurl the rock by impact of the winds,
With lightning rends and fires the sturdy oak,
They have no feeling of the crashing blows;
But I, I live and feel, my wounded heart
Appeals for aid to him who fashioned it.

Children of that Almighty Power, we stretch
Our hands in grief towards our common sire.
The vessel, truly, is not heard to say :
" Why should I be so vile, so coarse, so frail? "
Nor speech nor thought is given unto it.
The urn that, from the potter's forming hand,
Slips and is shattered has no living heart

[1] " Sub Deo justo nemo miser nisi mereatur. [Under a just God no one is miserable who has not deserved misery.] "— *St. Augustine.*

That yearns for bliss and shrinks from misery.
" This misery," ye say, " is others' good."
Yes; from my mouldering body shall be born
A thousand worms, when death has closed my pain.
Fine consolation this in my distress !
Grim speculators on the woes of men,
Ye double, not assuage, my misery.
In you I mark the nerveless boast of pride
That hides its ill with pretext of content.

I am a puny part of the great whole.
Yes; but all animals condemned to live,
All sentient things, born by the same stern law,
Suffer like me, and like me also die.

The vulture fastens on his timid prey,
And stabs with bloody beak the quivering limbs :
All's well, it seems, for it.   But in a while
An eagle tears the vulture into shreds;
The eagle is transfixed by shaft of man;
The man, prone in the dust of battlefield,
Mingling his blood with dying fellow men,
Becomes in turn the food of ravenous birds.
Thus the whole world in every member groans :
All born for torment and for mutual death.
And o'er this ghastly chaos you would say
The ills of each make up the good of all !
What blessedness !   And as, with quaking voice,
Mortal and pitiful, ye cry, " All's well,"
The universe belies you, and your heart
Refutes a hundred times your mind's conceit.

All dead and living things are locked in strife.
Confess it freely—evil stalks the land
Its secret principle unknown to us.
Can it be from the author of all good?
Are we condemned to weep by tyrant law
Of black Typhon or barbarous Ahriman ? [1]

[1] The Egyptian and Persian principles of evil.   The problem
is discussed in the following essay.—J. M.

These odious monsters, whom a trembling world
Made gods, my spirit utterly rejects.

But how conceive a God supremely good,
Who heaps his favours on the sons he loves,
Yet scatters evil with as large a hand?
What eye can pierce the depth of his designs?
From that all-perfect Being came not ill:
And came it from no other, for he's lord:
Yet it exists. O stern and numbing truth!
O wondrous mingling of diversities!
A God came down to lift our stricken race:
He visited the earth, and changed it not!
One sophist says he had not power to change;
"He had," another cries, "but willed it not:
In time he will, no doubt." And, while they prate,
The hidden thunders, belched from underground,
Fling wide the ruins of a hundred towns
Across the smiling face of Portugal.
God either smites the inborn guilt of man,
Or, arbitrary lord of space and time,
Devoid alike of pity and of wrath,
Pursues the cold designs he has conceived.
Or else this formless stuff, recalcitrant,
Bears in itself inalienable faults;
Or else God tries us, and this mortal life
Is but the passage to eternal spheres.
'Tis transitory pain we suffer here,
And death its merciful deliverance.
Yet, when this dreadful passage has been made,
Who will contend he has deserved the crown?
Whatever side we take we needs must groan;
We nothing know, and everything must fear.
Nature is dumb, in vain appeal to it,
The human race demands a word of God.
'Tis his alone to illustrate his work,
Console the weary, and illume the wise.
Without him man, to doubt and error doomed,
Finds not a reed that he may lean upon.

From Leibnitz learn we not by what unseen
Bonds, in this best of all imagined worlds,
Endless disorder, chaos of distress,
Must mix our little pleasures thus with pain;
Nor why the guiltless suffer all this woe
In common with the most abhorrent guilt.
'Tis mockery to tell me all is well.
Like learned doctors, nothing do I know.

Plato has said that men did once have wings
And bodies proof against all mortal ill;
That pain and death were strangers to their world.
How have we fallen from that high estate !
Man crawls and dies : all is but born to die :
The world's the empire of destructiveness.
This frail construction of quick nerves and bones
Cannot sustain the shock of elements;
This temporary blend of blood and dust
Was put together only to dissolve;
This prompt and vivid sentiment of nerve
Was made for pain, the minister of death :
Thus in my ear does nature's message run.
Plato and Epicurus I reject,
And turn more hopefully to learned Bayle.
With even poised scale Bayle bids me doubt.
He, wise enough and great to need no creed,
Has slain all systems—combats even himself :
Like that blind conqueror of Philistines,
He sinks beneath the ruin he has wrought.[1]
What is the verdict of the vastest mind ?
Silence : the book of fate is closed to us.
Man is a stranger to his own research;
He knows not whence he comes, nor whither goes.

[1] In a lengthy note Voltaire explains that Bayle never questioned Providence, and that the scepticism in which he follows Bayle is in regard to the source of evil. It will be seen from later pages, however, that Voltaire does not ascribe infinite power to his God. The words " all-perfect " and " almighty," which occur in this poem, are poetic phrases.— J. M.

Tormented atoms in a bed of mud,
Devoured by death, a mockery of fate.
But thinking atoms, whose far-seeing eyes,
Guided by thought, have measured the faint stars,
Our being mingles with the infinite;
Ourselves we never see, or come to know.
This world, this theatre of pride and wrong,
Swarms with sick fools who talk of happiness.
With plaints and groans they follow up the quest,
To die reluctant, or be born again.
At fitful moments in our pain-racked life
The hand of pleasure wipes away our tears;
But pleasure passes like a fleeting shade,
And leaves a legacy of pain and loss.
The past for us is but a fond regret,
The present grim, unless the future's clear.
If thought must end in darkness of the tomb,
All will be well one day—so runs our hope.
All *now* is well, is but an idle dream.
The wise deceive me : God alone is right.
With lowly sighing, subject in my pain,
I do not fling myself 'gainst Providence.
Once did I sing, in less lugubrious tone,
The sunny ways of pleasure's genial rule;
The times have changed, and, taught by growing
    age,
And sharing of the frailty of mankind,
Seeking a light amid the deepening gloom,
I can but suffer, and will not repine.

A caliph once, when his last hour had come,
This prayer addressed to him he reverenced :
" To thee, sole and all-powerful king, I bear
What thou dost lack in thy immensity—
Evil and ignorance, distress and sin."
He might have added one thing further—hope.

WE MUST TAKE SIDES;

OR, THE PRINCIPLE OF ACTION

INTRODUCTION

IT is not a question of taking sides between Russia and Turkey; for these States will, sooner or later, come to an understanding without my intervention.

It is not a question of declaring oneself in favour of one English faction and against another; for they will soon have disappeared, to make room for others.

I am not endeavouring to choose between Greek and Armenian Christians, Eutychians and Jacobites, Christians who are called Papists and Lutherans, Calvinists, Anglicans, the primitive folk called Quakers, Anabaptists, Jansenists, Molinists, Socinians, Pietists, and so many other 'ists. I wish to live in peace with all these gentlemen, whenever I may meet them, and never dispute with them; because there is not a single one of them who, when he has a crown to share with me, will not know his business perfectly, or who would spend a single penny for the salvation of my soul or his own.

I am not going to take sides between the old and the new French Parliaments; because in a few years there will be no question of either of them.

Nor between the ancients and the moderns; because the trial would be endless.

Nor between the Jansenists and the Molinists; because they exist no longer, and, thank God, five or six thousand volumes have become as useless as the works of St. Ephraim.

Nor between the partisans of the French and the Italian opera; because it is a mere matter of fancy.

The subject I have in mind is but a trifle—namely,

the question whether there is or is not a God; and I am going to examine it in all seriousness and good faith, because it interests me, and you also.

I

OF THE PRINCIPLE OF ACTION

Everything is in motion, everything acts and reacts, in nature.

Our sun turns on its axis with a rapidity that astonishes us; other suns turn with the same speed, while countless swarms of planets revolve round them in their orbits, and the blood circulates more than twenty times an hour in the lowliest of our animals.

A straw that is borne on the wind tends naturally towards the centre of the earth, just as the earth gravitates towards the sun, and the sun towards the earth. The sea owes to the same laws its eternal ebb and flow. In virtue of the same laws the vapours which form our atmosphere rise continually from the earth, and fall again in dew, rain, hail, snow, and thunder.

Everything, even death, is active. Corpses are decomposed, transformed into plants, and nourish the living, which in their turn are the food of others. What is the principle of this universal activity?

This principle must be unique. The unvarying uniformity of the laws which control the march of the heavenly bodies, the movements of our globe, every species and genus of animal, plant, and mineral, indicates that there is one mover. If there were two, they would either differ, or be opposed to each other, or like each other. If they were different, there would be no harmony; if opposed, things would destroy each other; if like, it would be as if there were only one—a twofold employment.

I am encouraged in this belief that there can be but one principle, one single mover, when I observe the constant and uniform laws of the whole of nature.

The same gravitation reaches every globe, and causes them to tend towards each other in direct proportion, not to their surfaces, which might be the effect of an impelling fluid, but to their masses.

The square of the revolution of every planet is as the cube of its distance from the sun (which proves, one may note, what Plato had somehow divined, that the world is the work of the eternal geometrician).

The rays of light are reflected and refracted from end to end of the universe. All the truths of mathematics must be the same on the star Sirius as in our little home.

If I glance at the animal world, I find that all quadrupeds, and all wingless bipeds, reproduce their kind by the same process of copulation, and all the females are viviparous.

All female birds lay eggs.

In each species there is the same manner of reproduction and feeding.

Each species of plants has the same basic qualities.

Assuredly the oak and the nut have come to no agreement to be born and to grow in the same way, any more than Mars and Saturn have come to an understanding to observe the same laws. There is, therefore, a single, universal, and powerful intelligence, acting always by invariable laws.

No one doubts that an armillary sphere, landscapes, drawings of animals, or models in coloured wax, are the work of clever artists. Is it possible for the copyists to be intelligent and the originals not? This seems to me the strongest demonstration; I do not see how it can be assailed.

II

OF THE NECESSARY AND ETERNAL PRINCIPLE OF ACTION

This single mover is very powerful, since it directs so vast and complex a machine. It is very intelligent, since the smallest spring of this machine cannot be equalled by us, who are intelligent beings.

It is a necessary being, since without it the machine would not exist.

It is eternal, for it cannot be produced from nothing, which, being nothing, can produce nothing; given the existence of something, it is demonstrated that something has existed for all eternity. This sublime truth has become trivial. So great has been the advance of the human mind in our time, in spite of the efforts to brutalise us which the masters of ignorance have made for so many centuries.

III
WHAT IS THIS PRINCIPLE?

I cannot prove synthetically the existence of the principle of action, the prime mover, the Supreme Being, as Dr. Clarke does. If this method were in the power of man, Clarke was, perhaps, worthy to employ it; but analysis seems to me more suitable for our poor ideas. It is only by ascending the stream of eternity that I can attempt to reach its source.

Having therefore recognised from movement that there is a mover; having proved from action that there is a principle of action; I seek the nature of this universal principle. And the first thing I perceive, with secret distress but entire resignation, is is that, being an imperceptible part of the great whole; being, as Plato says in the *Timaeus,* a point between two eternities; it will be impossible for me to understand this great whole, which hems me in on every side, and its master.

Yet I am a little reassured on seeing that I am able to measure the distance of the stars, and to recognise the course and the laws which keep them in their orbits. I say to myself: Perhaps, if I use my reason in good faith, I may succeed in discovering some ray of probability to lighten me in the dark

night of nature. And if this faint dawn which I seek
does not come to me, I shall be consoled to think
that my ignorance is invincible; that knowledge
which is forbidden me is assuredly useless to me;
and that the great Being will not punish me for having
sought a knowledge of him and failed to obtain it.

IV

WHERE IS THE FIRST PRINCIPLE?
IS IT INFINITE?

I do not see the first motive and intelligent
principle of the animal called man when he dem-
onstrates a geometrical proposition or lifts a burden.
Yet I feel irresistibly that there is one in him, however
subordinate. I cannot discover whether this first
principle is in his heart, or in his head, or in his
blood, or in his whole body. In the same way I have
detected a first principle in nature, and have seen
that it must necessarily be eternal. But where is it?

If it animates all existence, it is in all existence:
that seems to be beyond doubt. It is in all that exists,
just as movement is in the whole body of an animal,
if one may use so poor a comparison.

But while it is in what exists, can it be in what
does not exist? Is the universe infinite? I am told
that it is; but who will prove it? I regard it as eternal,
because it cannot have been made from nothing;
because the great principle, "nothing comes from
nothing," is as true as that two and two make four;
because, as we saw elsewhere, it is an absurd contradiction to say that the active being has spent an
eternity without acting, the formative being has been
eternal without forming anything, and the necessary
being has been, during an eternity, a useless being.

But I see no reason why this necessary being
should be infinite. Its nature seems to me to be
wherever there is existence; but why, and how, an
infinite existence? Newton has demonstrated the

void, which had until his time been a matter of con-
jecture. If there is a void in nature, there may be
a void outside nature. What need is there that beings
should extend to infinity? What would an infinite
extension be? Nor can we have infinity in number.
There is no number and no extension to which I
cannot add. It seems to me that in this matter the
conclusion of Cudworth is preferable to that of
Clarke.

God is present everywhere, says Clarke. Yes,
doubtless; but everywhere where there is something,
not where there is not. To be present in nothing seems
to me a contradiction in terms, an absurdity. I am
compelled to admit eternity, but I am not compelled
to admit an actual infinity.

In fine, what does it matter to me whether space
is a reality or merely an idea in my mind? What does
it matter whether or no the necessary, intelligent,
powerful, eternal being, the former of all being, is
in this imaginary space? Am I less his work? Am
I less dependent on him? Is he the less my master?
I see this master of the world with the eyes of my
mind, but I see him not beyond the world.

It is still disputed whether or no infinite space
is a reality. I will not base my judgment on so
equivocal a point, a quarrel worthy of the scholastics.
I will not set up the throne of God in imaginary
spaces.

If it is allowable to compare once more the little
things which seem large to us to what is great in
reality, let us imagine a gentleman of Madrid trying
to persuade a Castilian neighbour that the King of
Spain is master of the sea to the north of California,
and that whoever doubts it is guilty of high treason.
The Castilian replies: I do not even know whether
there is a sea beyond California. It matters little to
me whether there is or not, provided that I have the
means of subsistence in Madrid. I do not need this
sea to be discovered to make me faithful to the king

my master on the banks of the Manzanares. Whether
or no there are vessels beyond Hudson Bay, he has
none the less power to command me here; I feel my
dependence on him in Madrid, because I know that
he is master of Madrid.

In the same way, our dependence on the great
being is not due to the fact that he is present outside
the world, but to the fact that he is present in the
world. I do but ask pardon of the master of nature
for comparing him to a frail human being in order
to make my meaning clearer.

V

THAT ALL THE WORKS OF THE
ETERNAL BEING ARE ETERNAL

The principle of nature being necessary and eternal,
and its very essence being to act, it must have been
always active. If it had not been an ever-active God,
it would have been an eternally indolent God, the God
of Epicurus, the God who is good for nothing. This
truth seems to me to be fully demonstrated.

Hence the world, his work, whatever form it
assume, is, like him, eternal; just as the light is as
old as the sun, movement as old as matter, and food
as old as the animals; otherwise the sun, matter, and
the animals would be, not merely useless, but self-
contradictory things, chimaeras.

What, indeed, could be more contradictory than
an essentially active being that has been inactive
during an eternity; a formative being that has
fashioned nothing, or merely formed a few globes
some years ago, without there being the least apparent
reason for making them at one time rather than
another? The intelligent principle can do nothing
without reason; nothing can exist without an
antecedent and necessary reason. This antecedent and
necessary reason has existed eternally; therefore the
universe is eternal.

We speak here a strictly philosophical language; it is not our part even to glance at those who use the language of revelation.

VI

THAT THE ETERNAL BEING, AND FIRST PRINCIPLE, HAS ARRANGED ALL THINGS VOLUNTARILY.

It is clear that this supreme, necessary, active intelligence is possessed of will, and has arranged all things because it[1] willed them. How can one act, and fashion all things, without willing to fashion them? That would be the action of a mere machine, and this machine would presuppose another first principle, another mover. We should always have to end in a first intelligent being of some kind or other. We wish, we act, we make machines, when we will; hence the great very powerful *Demiourgos* has done all things because he willed.

Spinoza himself recognises in nature an intelligent, necessary power. But an intelligence without will would be an absurdity, since such an intelligence would be useless; it would do nothing, because it would not will to do anything. Hence the great necessary being has willed everything that it has done.

I said above that it has done all things necessarily because, if its works were not necessary, they would be useless. But does this necessity deprive it of will? Certainly not. I necessarily will to be happy, but I will it none the less on that account; on the contrary, I will it all the more strongly because I will it irresistibly.

Does this necessity deprive it of liberty? Not at

---

[1] Since the words "it" and "he" are both expressed by the French word "il," it is not clear whether Voltaire would have spoken of his supreme being as "it" or "he." I interpret his feeling as carefully as the context permits.—J. M.

all. Liberty can only be the power to act. Since the
supreme being is very powerful, it is the freest of
beings.

We thus recognise that the great artisan of things
is necessary, eternal, intelligent, powerful, possessed
of will, and free.

VII

THAT ALL BEINGS, WITHOUT EXCEPTION, ARE SUBJECT TO ETERNAL LAWS

What are the effects of this eternal power that
dwells essentially in nature? I see only two classes
of them, the insensitive and the sensitive.

The earth, the seas, the planets, the suns, seem
admirable but lifeless things, devoid of sensibility.
A snail that wills, has some degree of perception,
and makes love, seems, to that extent, to have an
advantage greater than all the glory of the suns that
illumine space.

But all these beings are alike subject to eternal
and unvarying laws.

Neither the sun, nor the snail, nor the oyster, nor
the dog, nor the ape, nor man, has given himself any
one of the things which he has; it is evident that they
have received everything.

Man and the dog are born, unwittingly, of a mother
who has brought them into the world in spite of
herself. Both of them suck the mother's breast without
knowing what they do, and they do this in virtue
of a very delicate and complex mechanism, the nature
of which is known to few men.

Both of them have, after a time, ideas, memory,
and will; the dog much earlier than the man.

If the animals were mere machines, it would be
another argument for the position of those who
believe that man also is a mere machine; but there
are now none who do not admit that the animals
have ideas, memory, and a measure of intelligence,

and that they improve their knowledge; that a hunting dog learns its work, an old fox is more astute than a young one, and so on.

Whence have they these faculties, if not from the primordial eternal cause, the principle of action, the great being that animates the whole of nature?

Man obtains the faculties of the animals much later than they, but in a higher degree; can he obtain them from any other source?

He has nothing but what the great being has given him. It would be a strange contradiction, a singular absurdity, if all the stars and elements, the animals and plants, obeyed, unceasingly and irresistibly, the laws of the great being, and man alone were independent of them.

VIII

THAT MAN IS ESSENTIALLY SUBJECT IN EVERYTHING TO THE ETERNAL LAWS OF THE FIRST PRINCIPLE

Let us regard, with the eyes of reason, this animal man which the great being has produced.

What is his first sensation? A sensation of pain; then the pleasure of feeding. That is the whole of our life: pain and pleasure. Whence have we these two springs which keep us in action until our last moment, if not from this first principle of action, this Demiourgos? Assuredly we do not give pain to ourselves; and how could we be the cause of our few pleasures? We have said elsewhere that it is impossible for us to invent a new kind of pleasure—that is to say, a new sense. Let us now say that it is equally impossible for us to invent a new kind of pain. The most execrable of tyrants cannot do it. The Jews, whose tortures have been described by the Benedictine monk Calmet in his dictionary, could only cut, tear, mutilate, draw, burn, strangle, and crush; all torments may thus be summarised. We can therefore do nothing of ourselves, either for good or evil; we are but the blind instruments of nature.

But I wish to think and I think, most men will recklessly assert. Let us consider it. What was our first idea after the feeling of pain? The idea of the breast that we sucked; then the face of the nurse; then a few other objects and needs made their faint impressions. Would anyone up to this point venture to say that he was more than a sentient automaton, a wretched abandoned animal destitute of knowledge or power, an outcast of nature? Will he venture to say that in this condition he is a thinking being, the author of his own ideas, the possessor of a soul? What is the son of a king when he leaves the womb? He would excite the disgust of his father, if he were not his father. A flower of the field that one treads underfoot is an infinitely superior thing.

IX

OF THE PRINCIPLE OF ACTION IN SENTIENT BEINGS

There comes at length a time when a greater or small number of perceptions, received in our mechanism, seem to present themselves to our will. We think that we are forming ideas. It is as if, when we turn the tap of a fountain, we were to think that we cause the water which streams out. We create ideas, poor creatures that we are! It is evident that we had no share in the former, yet we would regard ourselves as the authors of the latter. If we reflect well on this vain boast of forming ideas, we shall see that it is insolent and absurd.

Let us remember that there is nothing in external objects with the least analogy, the least relation, to a feeling, an idea, a thought. Let an eye or an ear be made by the best artisan in the world; the eye will see nothing, the ear will hear nothing. It is the same with our living body. The universal principle of action does everything in us. He has not made us an exception to the rest of nature.

Two experiences which are constantly repeated during the course of our life, and of which I have spoken elsewhere, will convince every thoughtful man that our ideas, our wills, and our actions do not belong to us.

The first is that no one knows, or can know, what idea he will have at any minute, what desire he will have, what word he will speak, what movement his body will perform.

The second is that during sleep it is clear that we have not the least share in what takes place in our dreams. We grant that we are then mere automata, on which an invisible power acts with a force that is as real and powerful as it is incomprehensible. This power fills the mind with ideas, inspires desires, passions, reflections. It sets in motion all the organs of the body. It has happened at times that a mother has smothered, in a restless dream, the new-born child that lay by her side; that a man has killed his friend. How many musicians have composed music during sleep? How many young preachers have composed sermons during their sleep?

If our life were equally divided between waking and sleeping, instead of our usually spending a third of our short career in sleep, and if we always dreamed during sleep, it would then be evident that half of our life did not depend on us. In any case, assuming that we spend eight out of the twenty-four hours in sleep, it is plain that a third of our existence is beyond our control. Add to this infancy, add all the time that is occupied in purely animal functions, and see how much is left. You will admit with surprise that at least half our life does not belong to us at all. Then reflect how inconsistent it would be if one half depended on us and the other half did not.

Conclude, therefore, that the universal principle of action does everything in us.

Here the Jansenist interrupts me and says: "You are a plagiarist; you have taken your doctrine from the famous book, *The Action of God on Created Things, or Physical Premotion,* by our great patriarch Boursier." I have said somewhere of Boursier that he had dipped his pen in the inkpot of the Deity. No, my friend; I have never received anything from the Jansenists or the Molinists except a strong aversion for sects, and some indifference to their opinions. Boursier, taking God as his model, knows precisely what was the nature of Adam's dream when God took a rib from his side wherewith to make woman; he knows the nature of his concupiscence, habitual grace, and actual grace. He knows, with St. Augustine, that men and women would have engendered children dispassionately in the earthly paradise, just as one sows a field, without any feeling of carnal pleasure. He is convinced that Adam sinned only by distraction in the earthly paradise. I know nothing about these things, and am content to admire those who have so splendid and profound a knowledge.

X

OF THE PRINCIPLE OF ACTION CALLED THE SOUL

But, some centuries later in the history of man, it came to be imagined that we have a soul which acts of itself; and the idea has become so familiar that we take it for a reality.

We talk incessantly of "the soul," though we have not the least idea of the meaning of it.

To some the soul means the life; to others it is a small, frail image of ourselves, which goes, when we die, to drink the waters of Acheron; to others it is a harmony, a memory, an entelechy. In the end it has been converted into a little being that is not body, a breath that is not air; and of this word "breath,"

which corresponds to "spirit" in many tongues, a kind
of thing has been made which is nothing at all.

Who can fail to see that men uttered, and still
utter, the word "soul" vaguely and without understanding, as we utter the words, "movement," "understanding," "imagination," "memory," "desire," and
"will"? There is no real being which we call will, desire,
memory, imagination, understanding, or movement;
but the real being called man understands, imagines,
remembers, desires, wills, and moves. They are
abstract terms, invented for convenience of speech.
I run, I sleep, I awake; but there is no such physical
reality as running, sleep, or awakening. Neither sight,
nor hearing, nor touch, nor smell, nor taste, is a real
being. I hear, I see, I smell, I taste, I touch. And
how could I do this if the great being had not so
disposed all things; if the principle of action, the
universal cause—in one word, God—had not given
us these faculties?

We may be quite sure that there would be just
as much reason to grant the snail a hidden being called
a "free soul" as to grant it to man. The snail has
a will, desires, tastes, sensations, ideas, and memory.
It wishes to move towards the material of its food
or the object of its love. It remembers it, has an idea
of it, advances towards it as quickly as it can; it knows
pleasure and pain. Yet you are not terrified when
you are told that the animal has not a spiritual soul;
that God has bestowed on it these gifts for a little
time; that he who moves the stars moves also the
insect. But when it comes to man you change your
mind. This poor animal seems to you so worthy of
your respect—that is to say, you are so proud—that
you venture to place in its frail body something that
seems to share the nature of God himself, yet
something that seems to you at times diabolical in
the perversity of its thoughts; something wise and
foolish, good and execrable, heavenly and infernal,
invisible, immortal, incomprehensible. And you have

familiarised yourself with this ideas, as you have grown accustomed to speak of movement, though there is no such being as movement; as you use abstract words, though there are no abstract beings.

XI

EXAMINATION OF THE PRINCIPLE OF ACTION CALLED THE SOUL

There is, nevertheless, a principle of action in man. Yes, there is one everywhere. But can this principle be anything else than a spring, a secret first mover which is developed by the ever-active first principle— a principle that is as powerful as it is secret, as demonstrable as it is invisible, which we have recognised as the essential cause in the whole of nature?

If you create movement or ideas because you will it, you are God for the time being; for you have all the attributes of God—will, power, and creation. Consider the absurdity into which you fall in making yourself God.

You have to choose between these two alternatives: either to be God whenever you will, or to depend continually on God. The first is extravagant; the second alone is reasonable.

If there were in our body a little god called "the free soul," which becomes so frequently a little devil, this little god would have to be regarded either as having been created from all eternity, or as created at the moment of your conception, or during your embryonic life, or at birth, or when you begin to feel. All these positions are equally ridiculous.

A little subordinate god, existing uselessly during a past eternity and descending into a body that often dies at birth, is the height of absurdity.

If this little god-soul is supposed to be created at the moment of conception, we must consider the master of nature, the being of beings, continually occupied in watching assignations, attentive to every intercourse of man and woman, every ready to dispatch a sentient and thinking soul into a recess between the entrails. A fine lodging for a little god! When the mother brings forth a still-born child, what becomes of the god-soul that had been lodged in the abdomen? Whither has it returned?

The same difficulties and absurdities, equally ridiculous and revolting, are found in connection with each of the other suppositions. The idea of a soul, as it is usually and thoughtlessly conceived by people, is one of the most foolish things that has ever been devised.

How much more reasonable, more decent, more respectful to the supreme being, more in harmony with our nature, and therefore truer, is it not to say:—

"We are machines made successively by the eternal geometrician; machines made like all the other animals, having the same organs, the same needs, the same pleasures, the same pains; far superior to all of them in many things, inferior to them in others; having received from the great being a principle of action which we cannot penetrate; receiving every-thing, giving ourselves nothing; and a million times more subject to him than the clay is to the potter who moulds it"?

Once more, either man is a god or he is precisely as I have described him.

XII

WHETHER THE PRINCIPLE OF ACTION IN ANIMALS IS FREE

There is a principle of action in man in every animal, just as there is in every machine; and this first mover, this ultimate spring, is necessarily eternally arranged by the master, otherwise all would be chaos, and there would be no world.

Every animal, like every machine, necessarily and irresistibly obeys the power that directs it. That is evident, and sufficiently familiar. Every animal is possessed of will, and one must be a fool to think that a dog following its master has not the will to follow him. No doubt, it follows him irresistibly; but it follows voluntarily. Does it follow freely? Yes, if nothing prevents it; that is to say, it can follow, it wills to follow, and it follows. The freedom to follow is not in its will, but in the power to walk that is given to it. A nightingale wills to make its nest, and makes it when it has found some moss. It had the freedom to construct this cradle, just as it had freedom to sing when it desires, and has not a chill. But was it free to have the desire? Did it will to will to make its nest? Had it that absurd "liberty of indifference" which theologians would describe as follows: "I neither will to make my nest nor the contrary; it is a matter of complete indifference to me; but I am going to will to make my nest solely for the sake of willing, and without being determined to do it in any way, merely to prove that I am free"? Such is the absurdity we find taught in the schools. If the nightingale could speak, it would say to these doctors: "I am irresistibly determined to nest, I will to nest, and I nest; you are irresistibly determined to reason badly, and you fulfil your destiny as I do mine."

We will now see if man is free in any other sense.

XIII

OF THE LIBERTY OF MAN, AND OF DESTINY

A ball that drives another, a hunting-dog that necessarily and voluntarily follows a stag, a stag that leaps a great ditch not less necessarily and voluntarily, a roe that gives birth to another roe, which will bring a third into the world—these things are not more irresistibly determined than we are to do all that we do. Let us remember always how inconsistent and absurd it would be for one set of things to be arranged and the other not.

Every present event is born of the past, and is father of the future; otherwise the universe would be quite other than it is, as Leibnitz has well said, more correct in this than in his pre-established harmony.[1] The eternal chain can be neither broken nor entangled. The great being who necessarily sustains it cannot let it hang uncertainly, nor change it; for he would then no longer be the necessary and immutable being, the being of beings; he would be frail, inconstant, capricious; he would belie his nature, and exist no longer.

Hence, an inevitable destiny is the law of nature, as the whole of antiquity felt. The dread of depriving man of some false liberty, robbing virtue of its merit, and relieving crime of its horror, has at times alarmed tender souls; but as soon as they were enlightened they returned to this great truth, that all things are enchained and necessary.

Man is free, we repeat, when he can do what he wills to do; but he is not free to will; it is impossible that he should will without cause. If this cause is not infallibly followed by its effect, it is no cause. It would not be more absurd for a cloud to say to the wind: "I do not wish to be driven by you." This truth can never injure morality. Vice is always vice, as disease is always disease. It will always be necessary to repress the wicked; if they are determined to evil, we must reply that they are equally predestined to chastisment.

Let us make these truths clearer.

---

[1] Leibnitz taught that material things never acted on each other; the only cause was God. The leaf fell from the tree, when the wind blew, because God had pre-established that coincidence, or harmony, of movements.—J. M.

XIV

ABSURDITY OF WHAT IS CALLED LIBERTY OF INDIFFERENCE

What an admirable spectacle is that of the eternal destinies of all beings chained to the throne of the maker of all worlds! I imagine a time when it is not so, but a chimerical liberty makes every event uncertain. I imagine that one of the substances intermediate between us and the great being (there may be millions of such beings) comes to consult the eternal being on the density of some of the enormous globes that stand at such vast distances from us. The sovereign of nature would be forced to reply: "I am not so sovereign, I am not the great necessary being; every little embryo is a master of destiny. The whole world is free to will without any other cause than the will. The future is uncertain; everything depends on caprice. I can foresee nothing. This great whole, which you regarded as so regular, is but a vast anarchy in which all is done without cause or reason. I shall be very careful not to say to you that such and such a thing will happen; for then the wicked folk who people the globes would do the contrary to what I had foretold, if it were only from malice. Men always dare to be jealous of their master, when he has not a power so absolute as to take away the very faculty of jealousy; they are pleased to see him fall into a trap. I am but weak and ignorant. Appeal to one more powerful and more gifted than I."

Possibly this allegory will avail more than any other argument to arrest the partisans of this empty liberty of indifference, if there still be any, and those who labour to reconcile foreknowledge with this liberty, and those who, in the university of Salamanca or in Bedlam, still speak of medicinal and concomitant grace.

XV

OF EVIL AND, IN THE FIRST PLACE, THE DESTRUCTION OF BEASTS

We have never had any idea of good and evil, save in relation to ourselves. The sufferings of an animal seem to us evils, because, being animals ourselves, we feel that we should excite compassion if the same were done to us. We should have the same feeling for a tree if we were told that it suffered torment when it was cut; and for a stone if we learned that it suffers when it is dressed. But we should pity the tree and the stone much less than the animal, because they are less like us. Indeed, we soon cease to be touched by the awful destiny of the beasts that are intended for our table. Children who weep at the death of the first chicken they see killed laugh at the death of the second.

It is only too sure that the disgusting carnage of our butcheries and kitchens does not seem to us an evil. On the contrary, we regard this horror, pestilential as it often is, as a blessing of the Lord; and we still have prayers in which we thank him for these murders. Yet what can be more abominable than to feed constantly on corpses?

Not only do we spend our lives in killing, and devouring what we have killed, but all the animals slaughter each other; they are impelled to do so by an invincible instinct. From the smallest insects to the rhinoceros and the elephant, the earth is but a vast battle-field, a world of carnage and destruction. There is no animal that has not its prey, and that, to capture it, does not employ some means equivalent to the ruse and rage with which the detestable spider entraps and devours the innocent fly. A flock of sheep devours in an hour, as it crops the grass, more insects than there are men on earth.

What is still more cruel is that in this horrible

scene of reiterated murder we perceive an evident
design to perpetuate all species by means of the bloody
corpses of their mutual enemies. The victims do not
expire until nature has carefully provided for new
representatives of the species. Everything is born
again to be murdered.

Yet I observe no moralist among us, nor any of
our fluent preachers or boasters, who has ever
reflected in the least on this frightful habit, which
has become part of our nature. We have to go back
to the pious Porphyry and the sympathetic Pytha-
goreans to find those who would shame us for our
bloody gluttony; or we must travel to the land of
the Brahmans. Our monks, the caprice of whose
founders has bade them renounce the flesh, are murderers of soles and turbots, if not the partridges and
quails. Neither among the monks, nor in the Council
of Trent, nor in the assemblies of the clergy, nor in
our academies, has this universal butchery ever been
pronounced an evil. There has been no more thought
given to it in the councils of the clergy than in our
public-houses.

Hence the great being is justified of these butcheries
in our eyes; or, indeed, we are his accomplices.

XVI

OF EVIL IN THE ANIMAL CALLED MAN

So much for the beasts; let us come to man. If
it be not an evil that the only being on earth that
knows God by his thoughts should be unhappy in
his thoughts; if it be not an evil that this worshipper
of the Deity should be almost always unjust and
suffering, should know virtue and commit crime,
should so often deceive and be deceived, and be the
victim or the executioner of his fellows, etc.; if all
that be not a frightful evil, I know not where evil
is to be found.

Beasts and men suffer almost without ceasing; men

suffer the more because, not only is the gift of thought often a source of torture, but this faculty of thinking always makes them fear death, which the beast cannot foresee. Man is a very miserable being, having but a few hours of rest, a few moments of satisfaction, and a long series of days of sorrow in his short life. Everybody admits and says this; and it is true.

They who have protested that all is well are charlatans. Shaftesbury, who set the fashion in this, was a most unhappy man. I have seen Bolingbroke torn with grief and rage; and Pope, whom he induced to put this miserable joke into verse, was one of the most pitiable men I have ever known, misshapen in body, unbalanced in temperament, always ill and a burden to himself, harassed by a hundred enemies until his last moment. At least let us have happy beings saying that all is well.

If by all is well it is merely meant that a man's head is happily placed above his shoulders, so that his eyes are better situated beside the root of his nose than behind his ears, we may assent. All is well in that sense. The laws of physics and mathematics are very well observed in his structure. A man who saw the beautiful Anne Boleyn, or the still more beautiful Mary Stuart, in her youth, would have said that it was well; would he have said it on seeing them die by the hand of the executioner? Would he have said it on seeing the grandson of the beautiful Mary Stuart perish in the same way in the heart of his capital? Would he have said it on seeing the great-grandson even more miserable, because he lived longer?

Glance over the human race, if it be but from the prescriptions of Sylla to the Irish massacres.

Behold these battle-fields, strewn by imbeciles with the corpses of other imbeciles, whom they have slain with a substance born of the experiments of a monk. See these arms, these legs, these bloody brains, and all these scattered limbs; it is the fruit of a quarrel between two ignorant ministers, neither of whom would dare to open his mouth in the presence of Newton, Locke, or Halley; or of some ridiculous quarrel between two forward women. Enter the neighbouring hospital, where are gathered those who are not yet dead. Their life is taken from them by fresh torments, and men make a fortune out of them, keeping a register of the victims who are dissected alive, at so much a day, under the pretext of healing them.

See these other men, dressed as comedians, earning a little money by singing, in a foreign language, a very obscure and insipid song, to thank the author of nature for this horrible outrage done to nature; and then tell me calmly that all is well.[1] Say the word, if you dare, in connection with Alexander VI. and Julius II.; say it over the ruins of a hundred towns that have been swallowed up by earthquakes, and amid the twelve millions of Americans who are being assassinated, in twelve million ways, to punish them for not being able to understand in Latin a papal bull that the monks have read to them. Say it to-day, the 24th of August, 1772; a day on which the pen trembles in my fingers, the two-hundred anniversay of the massacre of St. Bartholomew. Pass from these innumerable theatres of carnage to the equally unnumbered retreats of sorrow that cover the earth, to that swarm of diseases which slowly devour so many poor wretches while they yet live; think of that frightful ravage of nature which poisons the human race in its source, and associates the most abominable of plagues with the most necessary of pleasures. See that despised king Henry III., and that mediocre leader the Duke of Mayenne, struck down with the small-pox while they are waging civil war; and that insolent descendant of a Florentine merchant, Gondi, and Retz, the priest, archbishop of Paris preaching

---

[1] The allusion is to priests, in their coloured vestments, singing masses for a successful war.—J. M.

with sword in hand and body diseased. To complete this true and horrible picture, fancy yourself amid the floods and volcanoes that have so often devastated so many parts of the world; amid the leprosy and the plague that have swept it. And do you who read this recall all that you have suffered, admit that evil exists, and do not add to so many miseries and horrors the wild absurdity of denying them.

XVII

ROMANCES INVENTED TO EXPLAIN THE ORIGIN OF EVIL

Of a hundred who have sought the cause of physical and moral evil, the Hindoos are the first whose romantic imaginations are known to us. They are sublime, if the word "sublime" be taken to mean "high." Evil, according to the ancient Brahmans, comes of a quarrel that once took place in the highest heavens, between the faithful and the jealous angels. The rebels were cast out of heaven into Ondera for millions of ages. But the great being pardoned them at the end of a few thousand years; they were turned into men, and they brought upon the earth the evil that they had engendered in the empyraean. We have elsewhere described at length this ancient fable, the source of all fables.

It was finely imitated by gifted nations, and grossly reproduced by barbarians. Nothing, indeed, is more spiritual and agreeable than the story of Pandora and her box. If Hesiod has had the merit of inventing this allegory, I think it as superior to Homer as Homer is to Lycophron.

This box of Pandora, containing all the evils that have issued from it, seems to have all the charm of the most striking and delicate allusions. Nothing is more enchanting than this origin of our sufferings. But there is something still more admirable in the story of Pandora. It has a very high merit, which

seems to have escaped notice: it is that no one was
ever commanded to believe it.

XVIII

OF THE SAME ROMANCES, IMITATED BY
BARBARIC NATIONS

In the regions of Chaldaea and Syria the barbarians also had their legends of the origin of evil. Among
one of these nations in the neighbourhood of the
Euphrates it was said that a serpent, meeting a
burdened and thirsty ass, asked what the ass carried.
"The recipe of immortality," said the ass; "God has
bestowed it upon man, who has laid it on my back.
He follows me, but is far off, because he has only
two legs. I die of thirst; prithee tell me where there
is a stream." The serpent led the ass to water, and,
while it drank, stole the recipe. Hence it is that the
serpent is immortal, while man is subject to death
and all the pains that precede it.

You will observe that the serpent was thought by
all peoples to be immortal because it cast its skin.
If it changed its skin, this must have been in order
to become young again. I have spoken elsewhere of
this naïve theology; but it is well to bring it once
more to the notice of the reader, in order to show
him the nature of this venerable antiquity, in which
serpents and asses played such important parts.

The Syrians rose higher. They told that man and
woman, having been created in heaven, desired one
day to eat a certain cake; and that they then asked
an angel to show them the place of retirement. The
angel pointed to the earth. They went thither; and
God, to punish them for their gluttony, left them
there. Let us also leave them there, and their dinner
and their ass and their serpent. These inconceivable
puerilities of ancient Syria are not worth a moment's
notice. The detestable fables of an obscure people
should be excluded from a serious discussion.

Let us return from these miserable legends to the great saying of Epicurus, which has so long alarmed the whole earth, and to which there is no answer but a sigh: "Either God wished to prevent evil and could not do so; or he was able to do so, and did not wish."

A thousand bachelors and doctors of divinity have fired the arrows of the school at this unshakeable rock; in this terrible shelter have the Atheists taken refuge. Yet the Atheist must admit that there is in nature an active, intelligent, necessary, eternal principle and that from this principle comes all that we call good and evil. Let us discuss the point with the Atheist.

XIX

DISCOURSE OF AN ATHEIST ON ALL THIS

An Atheist says to me: It has been proved, I admit, that there is an eternal and necessary principle. But from the fact that it is necessary I infer that all that is derived from it is necessary; you have been compelled to admit this yourself. Since everything is necessary, evil is as inevitable as good. The great wheel of the ever-turning machine crushes all that comes in its way. I have no need of an intelligent being who can do nothing of himself, and who is as much a slave to his destiny as I am to mine. If he existed, I should have too much with which to reproach him. I should be obliged to call him either feeble or wicked. I would rather deny his existence than be discourteous to him. Let us get through this miserable life as well as we can, without reference to a fantastic being whom no one has ever seen, and to whom it would matter little, if he existed, whether we believed in him or not. What I think of him can no more affect him, supposing that he exists, than what he thinks of me, of which I am ignorant, affects me. There is no relation, no connection, no interest between him and me. Either there is no such being or he is an utter stranger to me. Let us do as nine

hundred and ninety-nine mortals out of a thousand
do; they work, generate, eat, drink, sleep, suffer, and
die, without speaking of metaphysics, or knowing that
there is such a thing.

XX

DISCOURSE OF A MANICHAEAN

A Manichaean, hearing the Atheist, says to him:
You are mistaken. Not only is there a God, but there
are necessarily two. It has been fully proved that the
universe is arranged intelligently, and there is an
intelligent principle in nature; but it is impossible that
this intelligent principle, which is the author of good,
should also be the author of evil. Evil must have its
own God. Zoroaster was the first to proclaim this
great truth, about two thousand years ago; and two
other Zoroasters came afterwards to confirm it. The
Parsees have always followed, and still follow, this
excellent doctrine. Some wretched people or other,
called the Jews, at that time in bondage to us, learned
a little of our science, together with the names of
Satan and Knatbull. They recognised God and the
devil; and the devil was so powerful, in the opinion
of this poor little people, that one day, when God
had descended into their country, the devil took him
up into a mountain. Admit two gods, therefore; the
world is large enough to hold them and find sufficient
work for them.

XXI

DISCOURSE OF A PAGAN

Then a Pagan arose, and said: If we are to admit
two gods, I do not see what prevents us from worshipping a thousand. The Greeks and Romans, who
were superior to you, were polytheists. It will be
necessary some day to return to the admirable
doctrine that peoples the universe with genii and

deities; it is assuredly the only system which explains everything—the only one in which there is no contradiction. If your wife betrays you, Venus is the cause of it. If you are robbed, put the blame on Mercury. If you lose an arm or a leg in battle, it was arranged by Mars. So much for the evil. In regard to the good, not only do Apollo, Ceres, Pomona, Bacchus, and Flora load you with presents, but occasionally the same Mars will rid you of your enemies, the same Venus will find you mistresses, the same Mercury may pour all your neighbours' gold into your coffers, provided your hand comes to the assistance of his wand.

It was much easier for these gods to agree in governing the universe than it seems to be to this Manichaean to reconcile his Ormuzd, the benevolent, and Ahriman, the malevolent, two mortal enemies, so as to maintain both light and darkness. Many eyes see better than one. Hence all the poets of antiquity are continually calling councils of the gods. How can you suppose that one god is enough to see to all the details of life on Saturn and all the business of the star Capella? What! You imagine that everything on our globe, except in the houses of the King of Prussia and the Pope Ganganelli, is regulated by councils, and there is no council in heaven! There is no better way of deciding things than by a majority of votes. The deity always acts in the wisest way. The Theist seems to me, in comparison with a pagan, to be like a Prussian soldier entering the territory of Venice; he is charmed with the excellence of the government. "The king of this country," he says, "must work from morning to night. I greatly pity him." "There is no king," people reply; " we are governed by a council."

Here are the true principles of our ancient religion.

The great being known as Jehovah or Yaa among the Phoenicians, the Jove of other Asiatic nations,

the Jupiter of the Romans, the Zeus of the Greeks,
is the sovereign of gods and men.

Deum sator atque hominum rex.

The master of the whole of nature, to whom nothing
in the whole range of being approaches.

Cui nihil simile, nec secundum.

The animating spirt of the universe.

Jovis omnia plena.

All the ideas that one may have of God are enfolded
in this fine verse of the ancient Orpheus, quoted
throughout antiquity, and repeated in all the
mysteries.

εἰς ἔστ', αὐτογενής, ἑνὸς ἔκγονα πάντα τέτυκται.

"He is One, self-born, and all was born of One."

But he confides to the subordinate gods the care
of the stars, the elements, the seas, and the bowels
of the earth. His wife, who represents the expanse
of space that he fills, is Juno. His daughter, who is
eternal wisdom, his word, is Minerva. His other
daughter, Venus, is the lover of the poetical
generation. She is the mother of love, inflaming all
sensitive beings, uniting them, reproducing by the
attraction of pleasure all that necessity devotes to
death. All the gods have made presents to mortals.
Ceres has given them corn, Bacchus the vine, Pomona
fruit; Apollo and Mercury have taught them the arts.

The great Zeus, the great Demiourgos, had made
the planets and the earth. He had brought men and
animals into existence on our planet. The first man
was, according to the account of Berosus, Alora,
father of Sares, grandfather of Alaspara, who begot
Amenon, of whom was born Metalare, who was the
father of Daon, father of Everodao, father of Amphis,
father of Osiarte, father of the famous Sixutros or
Xixutrus, King of Chaldaea, under whom occurred
the well-known deluge, which the Greeks called "the

deluge of Ogyges"; a flood of which the precise date
is still uncertain, as is that of the other great inunda-
tion, which swallowed up the isle of Atlantis and part
of Greece about six thousand years ago.

We have another theogony in Sanchoniathon,
without a deluge. Those of the Hindoos, Chinese, and
Egyptians are very different again.

All events of antiquity are lost in a dark night;
but the existence and blessings of Jupiter are clearer
than the light of the sun. The hero who, stirred by
his example, did good to men was known by the
holy name of Dionysos, son of God. Bacchus,
Hercules, Perseus, and Romulus also received this
divine name. Some went so far even as to say that
the divine virtue was communicated to their mothers.
The Greeks and Romans, although they were
somewhat debauched, as are to-day all Christians
of a sociable nature, rather drunken, like the canons
of Germany, and given to unnatural vices, like the
French king Henry III. and his Nogaret, were very
religious. They offered sacrifice and incense, walked
in processions, and fasted.

But everything becomes corrupt in time. Religion
changed. The splendid name of Son of God—that
is to say, just and benevolent—was afterwards given
to the most unjust and cruel of men, because they
were powerful. The ancient piety, which was humane,
was displaced by superstition, which is always cruel.
Virtue had dwelt on the earth as long as the fathers
of families were the only priests, and offered to Jupiter
and the immortal gods the first of their fruits and
flowers; but all this was changed when the priests
began to shed blood and wanted to share with the
gods. They did share in truth; they took the offerings,
and left the smoke to the gods. You know how our
enemies succeeded in crushing us, adopting our earlier
morals, rejecting our bloody sacrifices, calling men
to the Church, making a party for themselves among
the poor until such time as they should capture the

rich. They took our place. We are annihilated, they triumph; but, corrupted, at length like ourselves, they need a great reform, which I wish them with all my heart.

XXII
DISCOURSE OF A JEW

Take no notice of this idolatrous pagan who would turn God into a Dutch president, and offer us subordinate gods like members of parliament.

My religion, being above nature, can have no resemblance to others.

The first difference between them and us is that the source of our religion was hidden for a very long time from the rest of the earth. The dogmas of our fathers were buried, like ourselves, in a little country about a hundred and fifty miles long and sixty in width. In this well dwelt the truth that was unknown to the whole world, until certain rebels, going forth from among us, took from it the name of "truth" in the reigns of Tiberius, Caligula, Claudius, and Nero; and presently boasted that they were establishing a new truth.

The Chaldaeans recognised Alora as their father, as you know. The Phoenicians descended from a man named Origen, according to Sanchoniathon. The Greeks had their Prometheus; the Atlantids had their Ouran, called in Greek Ouranos. I say nothing of the Chinese, Hindoos, or Scythians. We had our Adam, of whom nobody ever heard except our nation, and we only very late. It was not the Hephaistos of the Greeks, known to the Latins as Vulcan, who invented the art of using metals; it was Tubalcain. The whole of the West was astonished to hear, under Constantine, that it was not Bacchus to whom the nations owed the use of wine, but Noah, whose name none knew in the whole Roman Empire, any more than they knew the names of his ancestors, which were unknown throughout the earth. The anecdote was learned only from our Bible, when it was translated into Greek; it began to spread about that time. The sun was then seen to be no longer the source of light; the light was created before the sun, and separated from the darkness, as the waters were separated from the waters. Woman was made from a rib, which God himself took out of a sleeping man, without awakening him, and without causing his descendants to be short of a rib.

The Tigris, Araxis, Euphrates, and Nile all had their source in the same garden. We do not know where the garden was, but its existence is proved, because the gate was guarded by a cherub.

Animals speak. The eloquence of a serpent was fatal to the whole human race. A Chaldaean prophet conversed with his ass.

God, the creator of all men, is not the father of all men, but of one family alone. This family, always wandering, left the fertile land of Chaldaea to wander for some time in the neighbourhood of Sodom; from this journey it acquired an incontestable right to the city of Jerusalem, which was not yet in existence.

Our family increases at such a rate that seventy men produce, at the end of two hundred and fifty years, six hundred and thirty thousand men bearing arms; counting the women, children, and old men, that amounts to about three millions. These three millions live in a small canton of Egypt which cannot maintain twenty thousand people. For their advantage God puts to death in one night all the first-born of the Egyptians; and, after this massacre, instead of giving Egypt to his people, God puts himself at their head to fly with them dry-foot across the sea, and cause a whole generation of Jews to die in the desert.

We have seven times been in slavery in spite of the appalling miracles that God works for us every day, causing the moon to stand still in midday, and also the sun. Ten out of twelve of our tribes perished

for ever. The other two are scattered and in misery.
We have always prophets, nevertheless. God descends
continually among our people alone, and mingles only
with us. He appears constantly to these prophets, his
sole confidants and favourites.

He goes to visit Addo or Iddo or Jeddo, and commands him to travel without eating. The prophet
things that God has ordered him to eat that he may
walk better (I Kings xiii.).

God commands Isaiah to go forth among his fellow
citizens in a most unbecoming state of attire, *disco-
opertis natibus* (Isaiah xx.).

God orders Jeremiah to put a yoke on his neck
and a saddle on his back (ch. xxvii. according to the
Hebrews).

He orders Ezekiel to have himself bound, to eat
a parchment book, to lie for two hundred and ninety
days on the right side and forty days on the left side,
and then to eat filth with his bread.

He commands Hosea to take a prostitute and have
three children by her; then he commands him to pay
an adulterous woman and have children by her.

Add to all these prodigies an uninterrupted series
of massacres, and you will see that among us all things
are divine, because nothing is in accordance with what
men call decent laws.

Unhappily, we were not well known to other
nations until we were nearly annihilated. It was our
enemies, the Christians, who made us known when
they despoiled us. They built up their system with
material taken from a bad Greek translation of our
Bible. They insult and oppress us to this day; but
our turn will come. It is well known how we will
triumph at the end of the world, when there will be
no one left on the earth.

XXIII
DISCOURSE OF A TURK

When the Jew had finished, a Turk, who had smoked throughout the meeting, washed his mouth, recited the formula "Allah Illah," and said to me:—

I have listened to all these dreamers. I have gathered that thou art a dog of a Christian, but thou pleasest me because thou seemest liberal, and art in favour of gratuitous predestination. I believe thou art a sensible man, assuming that thou dost agree with me.

Most of thy dogs of Christians have spoken only folly about our Mohammed. A certain Baron de Tott, a man of much ability and geniality, who did us great service in the last war, induced me some time ago to read a book of one of your most learned men, named Grotius, entitled *The Truth of the Christian Religion.* This Grotius accuses our great Mohammed of forcing men to believe that a pigeon spoke in his ear, that a camel conversed with him during the night, and that he had put half the moon in his sleeve. If the most learned of your Christ-worshippers can write such asinine stuff, what must I think of the others?

No, Mohammed did none of these village-miracles, of which people speak only a hundred years after the supposed event. He wrought none of those miracles which Baron de Tott read to me in the *Golden Legend,* written at Geneva. He wrought none of your miracles in the manner of St. Médard, which have been so much derided in Europe, and at which a French ambassador has laughed so much in our presence. The miracles of Mohammed were victories. God has shown that he was a favourite by subjecting half our hemisphere to him. He was not unknown for two whole centuries. He triumphed as soon as he was persecuted.

His religion is wise, severe, chaste, and humane. Wise, because it knows not the folly of giving God associates, and it has no mysteries; severe, because it prohibits games of chance, and wine, and strong drinks, and orders prayer five times a day; chaste, because it reduces to four the prodigious number of spouses who shared the bed of all oriental princes; humane, because it imposes on us almsgiving more rigorously than the journey to Mecca.

Add tolerance to all these marks of truth. Reflect that we have in the city of Stamboul alone more than a hundred thousand Christians of all sects, who carry out all the ceremonies of their cults in peace, and live so happily under the shelter of our laws that they never deign to visit you, while you crowd to our imperial gate.

XXIV

DISCOURSE OF A THEIST

A Theist then asked permission to speak, and said:—

Everyone has his own opinion, good or bad. I should be sorry to distress any good man. First, I ask pardon of the Atheist; but it seems to me that, compelled as he is to admit an excellent design in the order of the universe, he is bound to admit an intelligence that has conceived and carried out this design. It is enough, it seems to me, that, when the Atheist lights a candle, he admits that it is for the purpose of giving light. It seems to me that he should also grant that the sun was made to illumine our part of the universe. We must not dispute about such probable matters.

The Atheist should yield the more graciously since, being a good man, he has nothing to fear from a master who has no interest in injuring him. He may quite safely admit a God; he will not pay a penny the more in taxes, and will not live less comfortably.

As to you, my pagan friend, I submit that you are rather late with your project of restoring poly-theism. For that Maxentius ought to have defeated Constantine or else Julian ought to have lived thirty years longer.

I confess that I see no impossibility in the existence of several beings far superior to us, each of whom would superintend some heavenly body. Indeed, it would give me some pleasure to prefer your Naiads, Dryads, Sylvans, Graces, and Loves to St. Fiacre, St. Pancratius, Sts. Crepin and Crepinien, St. Vitus, St. Cunegonde, or St. Marjolaine. But, really, one must not multiply things without need; and as a single intelligence suffices for the regulation of the world, I will stop at that until other powers show me that they share its rule.

As to you, my Manichaean friend, you seem to me a duellist, very fond of fighting. I am a peaceful man, and do not like to find myself between two rivals who are ever at war. Your Ormuzd is enough for me; you can keep your Ahriman.

I shall always be somewhat embarrassed in regard to the origin of evil; but I suppose that the good Ormuzd, who made everything, could not do better. I cannot offend him if I say to him: You have done all that a powerful, wise, and good being could do. It is not your fault if your works cannot be as good and perfect as yourself. Imperfection is one of the essential differences between you and your creatures. You could not make gods; it was necessary that, since men possessed reason, they should display folly, just as there must be friction in every machine. Each man has his dose of imperfection and folly, from the very fact that you are perfect and wise. He must not be always happy, because you are always happy. It seems to me that a collection of muscles, nerves, and veins cannot last more than eighty or a hundred years at the most, and that you must be for ever. It seems to me impossible that an animal, necessarily compacted of desires and wills, should not at times wish to serve his own purpose by doing evil to his neighbour. You only never do evil. Lastly, there is necessarily so great a distance between you and your works that the good is in you, and the evil must be in them.[1]

As for me, imperfect, as I am, I thank you for giving me a short span of existence, and especially for not having made me a professor of theology.

That is not at all a bad compliment. God could not be angry with me, seeing that I do not wish to displease him. In fine, I feel that, if I do no evil to my brethren and respect my master, I shall have nothing to fear, either from Ahriman, or Cerberus and the Furies, or Satan, or Knatbull, or St. Fiacre and St. Crepin; and I shall end my days in peace and the pursuit of philosophy.

I come now to you, Mr. Abrabanel and Mr. Benjamin.[2] You seem to me to be the maddest of the lot. The Kaffirs, Hottentots, and blacks of New Guinea are more reasonable and decent beings than your Jewish ancestors were. You have surpassed all nations in exorbitant legends, bad conduct, and barbarism. You are paying for it; it is your destiny. The Roman Empire has fallen; the Parsees, your former masters, are scattered. The Armenians sell rags, and occupy a low position in the whole of Asia. There is no trace left of the ancient Egyptians. Why should you be a power?

---

[1] Voltaire always candidly faces the problem of evil, and admits that it is inconsistent with infinite power and goodness. In another treatise he makes the bold observation that, since morality is merely a social law regulating the relations of men, it has no application to his isolated "great being."—J. M.

[2] Well-known Jews in mediaeval history.—J. M.

As to you, my Turkish friend, I advise you to come to terms as soon as possible with the Empress of Russia, if you wish to keep what you have usurped in Europe. I am willing to believe that the victories of Mohammed, son of Abdala, were miracles; but Catherine II. also works miracles. Take care that she do not some day perform the miracle of sending you back to the deserts from which you came. In particular, continue to be tolerant; it is the true way to please the being of beings, who is alike the father of Turks and Russians, Chinese and Japanese, black and yellow man, and of the whole of nature.

XXV
DISCOURSE OF A CITIZEN

When the Theist had spoken, a man arose and said: I am a citizen, and therefore the friend of all these gentlemen. I will not dispute with any of them. I wish only to see them all united in the design of aiding and loving each other, in making each other happy, in so far as men of such different opinions can love each other, and contribute to each other's happiness, which is as difficult as it is necessary.

To attain this end, I advise them first to cast in the fire all the controversial books which come their way, especially those of the Jesuits; and also the ecclesiastical gazette, and all other pamphlets which are but the fuel of the civil war of fools.

Next, each of our brethren, whether Theist, Turk, Pagan, Greek Christian, Latin Christian, Anglican, Scandinavian, Jew, or Atheist, will read attentively several pages of Cicero's *De Officiis,* or of Montaigne, and some of La Fontaine's *Fables.*

The reading of these works insensibly disposes men to that concord which theologians have hitherto held in horror. Their minds being thus prepared, every time that a Christian and a Mussulman meet an Atheist they will say to him: "Dear brother, may heaven enlighten you"; and the Atheist will reply: "When I am converted I shall come and thank you."

The Theist will give two kisses to the Manichaean woman in honour of the two principles. The Greek and Roman woman will give three to each member of the other sects, even the Quakers and Jansenists. The Socinians need only embrace once, seeing that those gentlemen believe there is only one person in God; but this embrace will be equal to three when it is performed in good faith.

We know that an Atheist can live very cordially with a Jew, especially if the Jew does not charge more than eight per cent. in lending him money; but we have no hope of ever seeing a lively friendship between a Calvinist and a Lutheran. All that we require of the Calvinist is that he return the salute of the Lutheran with some affection, and do not follow the example of the Quakers, who do reverence to nobody; but the Calvinists have not their candour.

We urge the primitive folk called Quakers to marry their sons to the daughters of the Theists who are known as Socinians, as these young ladies, being nearly all the daughters of priests, are very poor. Not only will it be a very good deed before God and men, but these marriages will produce a new race, which, representing the first years of the Christian Church, will be very useful to the human race.

These preliminaries being settled, if any quarrel occur between members of two different sects, they must never choose a theologian as arbitrator, for he would infallibly eat the oyster and leave them the shells.

To maintain the established peace nothing shall be offered for sale, either by a Greek to a Turk, a Turk to a Jew, or a Roman to a Roman, except what pertains to food, clothing, lodging, or pleasure. They shall not sell circumcision, or baptism, or burial, or permission to turn round the black stone in the *caaba,* or to harden one's kness before Our Lady of Loretto, who is still blacker.

In all the disputes that shall arise it is expressly forbidden to treat any person as a dog, however angry one may be—unless indeed we treat dogs as men when they steal our dinner or bite us.

THE QUESTIONS OF ZAPATA

(TRANSLATED BY DR. TAMPONET, OF THE SORBONNE.)

The licentiate Zapata, being appointed Professor of Theology at the University of Salamanca, presented these questions to a committee of doctors in 1629. They were suppressed. The Spanish copy is in the Brunswick Library.

WISE MASTERS,

1°. How ought I to proceed with the object of showing that the Jews, whom we burn by the hundred, were for four thousand years God's chosen people?

2°. How could God, whom one cannot without blasphemy regard as unjust, forsake the whole earth for the little Jewish tribe, and then abandon this little group for another, which, during two hundred years, was even smaller and more despised?

3°. Why did he perform a number of incomprehensible miracles in favour of this miserable nation before the period which is called *historical*? Why did he, some centuries ago, cease to perform them? And why do we, who are God's people, never witness any?

4°. If God is the God of Abraham, why do you burn the children of Abraham? And, when you burn them, why do you recite their prayers? How is it that, since you worship the book of their law, you put them to death for observing that law?

5°. How shall I reconcile the chronology of the Chinese, Chaldæans, Phœnicians, and Egyptians with that of the Jews? And how shall I reconcile the forty different methods of calculation which I find in the commentators? If I say that God dictated the book,

48

I may be told that God evidently is not an expert in chronology.

6°. By what argument can I prove that the books attributed to Moses were written by him in the desert? How could he say that he wrote beyond the Jordan when he never crossed the Jordan? I may be told that God is evidently not good at geography.

7°. The book entitled *Joshua* says that Joshua had Deuteronomy engraved on stones coated with mortar; this passage in *Joshua*, and others in ancient writers, clearly prove that in the days of Moses and Joshua the peoples of the East engraved their laws and observations on stone and brick. The Pentateuch tells us that the Jewish people were without food and clothing in the desert; it seems hardly probable that, if they had no tailors or shoemakers, they had men who were able to engrave a large book. In any case, how did they preserve this large work inscribed in mortar?

8°. What is the best way to refute the objections of the learned men who find in the Pentateuch the names of towns which were not yet in existence; precepts for kings whom the Jews detested, and who did not reign until seven hundred years after Moses; and passages in which the author betrays that he was much later than Moses, as: " The bed of Og, which is still seen in Ramath," " The Canaanite was then in the land," etc., etc., etc., etc.?

These learned men might, with the difficulties and contradictions which they impute to the Jewish chronicles, give some trouble to a licentiate.

9°. Is the book of *Genesis* to be taken literally or allegorically? Did God really take a rib from Adam and make woman therewith? and, if so, why is it previously stated that he made man male and female? How did God create light before the sun? How did he separate light from darkness, since darkness is merely the absence of light? How could there be a day before the sun was made? How was the firmament made amid the waters, since there is no such thing as a firmament—it is an illusion of the ancient Greeks? There are those who suggest that *Genesis* was not written until the Jews had some knowledge of the erroneous philosophy of other peoples, and it would pain me to hear it said that God knows no more about physics than he does about chronology and geography.

10°. What shall I say of the garden of Eden, from which issued a river which divided into four rivers— the Tigris, Euphrates, Phison (which is believed to be the Phasis), and Gihon, which flows in Ethiopia, and must therefore be the Nile, the source of which is a thousand miles from the source of the Euphrates? I shall be told once more that God is a very poor geographer.

11°. I should, with all my heart, like to eat the fruit which hung from the tree of knowledge; and it seems to me that the prohibition to eat it is strange. Since God endowed man with reason, he ought to encourage him to advance in knowledge. Did he wish to be served only by fools? I should also like to have speech with the serpent, since it was so intelligent; but I should like to know what language it spoke. The Emperor Julian, a great philosopher, asked this of the great St. Cyril, who could not meet the question, and said to the learned emperor : " You are the serpent." St. Cyril was not polite; but you will observe that he did not perpetrate this theological impertinence until Julian was dead.

Genesis says that the serpent eats earth; you know that *Genesis* is wrong, and that earth alone contains no nourishment. In regard to God walking familiarly every day in the garden, and talking to Adam and Eve and the serpent, I may say that it would have been very pleasant to have been there. But as I think you are much more fitted for the kind of society which Joseph and Mary had in the stable at Bethlehem, I will not advise you to visit the Garden of Eden, especially as the gate is now guarded by a

cherub armed to the teeth.   It is true that, according
to the rabbis, *cherub* means " ox." [1]   A curious kind
of porter !   Please let me know at least what a
cherub is.

12°.   How shall I explain the story of the angels
who fell in love with the daughters of men, and begot
giants?   May I not be told that this episode is borrowed from pagan legends?   But as the Jews invented everything in the desert, and were very
ingenious, it is clear that all the other nations took
their science from the Jews.   Homer, Plato, Cicero,
and Vergil learned all they knew from the Jews.   Is
not that proved?

13°.   How shall I get out of the deluge, the cataracts
of heaven (which has no cataracts), and the animals
coming from Japan, Africa, America, and the south,
and being enclosed in a large ark with food and drink
for one year, without counting the time when the
earth was still too damp to produce food for them?
How did Noah's little family manage to give all these
animals their proper food?   It consisted only of
eight persons.

14°.   How can I make the story of the tower of
Babel plausible?   This tower must have been higher
than the pyramids of Egypt, since God allowed the
building of the pyramids.   Did it reach as high as
Venus, or at least to the moon?

15°.   By what device shall I justify the two lies of
Abraham, the father of believers, who, at the age of
one hundred and thirty-five (counting carefully),
represented the pretty Sarah as his sister in Egypt
and at Gerar, in order that the kings of those countries
might fall in love with her and make presents to
him?   What a naughty thing to do, to sell one's
wife !

16°.   Give me some explanation why, although God

[1] The *kerubim* (or " cherubim ") of the Old Testament are
the winged bulls of the ancient Babylonians, of which there
are two fine specimens in the British Museum.—J. M.

told Abraham that all his posterity should be circumcised, this was not done under Moses.

17°. Can I know by my natural powers whether the three angels, to whom Sarah offered a whole calf to eat, had bodies, or borrowed bodies?

18°. Will my hearers believe me when I tell them that Lot's wife was changed into a salt statue? What shall I say to those who tell me that it is probably a coarse imitation of the ancient fable of Eurydice, and that a salt statue would not last in the rain?

19°. What shall I say in justification of the blessings which fell on Jacob, the just man, who deceived his father Isaac and robbed his father-in-law Laban? How shall I explain God appearing to him at the top of a ladder? And how could Jacob fight an angel all night?, etc., etc.

20°. How must I treat the sojourn of the Jews in Egypt and their escape? *Exodus* says that they remained four hundred years in Egypt; but, counting carefully, we find only two hundred and five years. Why did Pharaoh's daughter bathe in the Nile, in which no one ever bathes on account of the crocodiles?, etc., etc.

21°. Moses having wedded the daughter of an idolater, how could God choose him as his prophet without reproaching him? How could Pharaoh's magicians work the same miracles as Moses, except that of covering the land with lice and vermin? How could they change into blood all the waters, since these had already been changed into blood by Moses? How was it that Moses, led by God himself, and at the head of six hundred and thirty thousand fighting men, fled with his people, instead of taking Egypt, in which God had slain all the first-born? Egypt never had an army of a hundred thousand men, from the first mention of it in historical times. How was it that Moses, flying with his troops from the land of Goshen, crossed half of Egypt, instead of going straight to Canaan, and advanced as far as Memphis,

between Baal-Sephon and the Red Sea? Finally,
how could Pharaoh pursue him with all his cavalry
when, in the fifth plague of Egypt, God had just
destroyed all the horses and beasts in the country,
and, moreover, Egypt, which is much broken by canals,
always had very little cavalry?

22°. How shall I reconcile what is said in *Exodus*
with the speech of St. Stephen in *Acts* and the passages of *Jeremiah* and *Amos*? *Exodus* says that they
sacrificed to Jehovah for forty years in the desert;
Jeremiah, Amos, and St. Stephen say that neither
sacrifice nor victim was offered during all that time.
Exodus says that they made the tabernacle, which
contained the ark of the covenant; St. Stephen, in
Acts, says that they took the tabernacle from Moloch
and Remphan.

23°. I am not sufficiently versed in chemistry to
deal happily with the golden calf which, *Exodus* says,
was made in a day, and which Moses reduced to ashes.
Are they two miracles, or two possibilities of human
art?

24°. Was it a further miracle for the leader of a
nation, in a desert, to have twenty-three thousand men
of that nation slain by a single one of the twelve
tribes, and for twenty-three thousand men to let
themselves be massacred without making any
defence?

25°. Must I again regard it as a miracle, or as an
act of ordinary justice, that twenty-four thousand
Hebrews were put to death because one of them had
lain with a Midianite woman, while Moses himself
had married a Midianite? And were not these
Hebrews, who are described to us as so ferocious,
really very good fellows to let themselves be slain for
girls?

26°. What explanation shall I give of the law which
forbids the eating of the hare " because it ruminates,
and has not a cloven foot," whereas hares have cloven
feet and do not ruminate? We have already seen

that this remarkable book suggests that God is a poor geographer, a poor chronologist, and a poor physicist; he seems to have been no less weak in natural history. How can I explain other equally wise laws, such as that of the waters of jealousy and the sentence of death on a man who lies with his wife during the menstrual period?, etc., etc., etc. Can I justify these barbaric and ridiculous laws, which are said to have been given by God himself?

27°. What answer shall I make to those who are surprised that a miracle was needed to effect the crossing of the Jordan, since it is only forty-five feet across at its widest, could easily be crossed with a small raft, and was fordable at many points, as we learn from the slaying of forty-two thousand Ephraimites by their brothers at a ford of the same river?

28°. What reply shall I make to those who ask how the walls of Jericho fell at the sound of a trumpet, and why other towns did not fall in the same way?

29°. How shall I excuse the conduct of the harlot Rahab in betraying her country, Jericho? How was this treachery necessary, since they had only to blow their trumpet to take a town? And how shall I fathom the depth of the divine decrees which enacted that our divine Saviour Jesus Christ should descend from this harlot Rahab, from the incest of Thamar with her father-in-law Judah, and from the adultery of David and Bathsheba? How incomprehensible are the ways of God!

30°. How can I approve of Joshua hanging thirty-one kinglets and usurping their little States—that is to say, their villages?

31°. How shall I speak of the battle of Joshua with the Amorites at Beth-horon on the way to Gibeon? The Lord sends a rain of stones, from Beth-horon to Azekah: it is fifteen miles from Bath-horon to Azekah; therefore the Amorites were exterminated by rocks which fell from heaven over a space of fifteen miles. The Scripture says that it was midday.

Why, then, did Joshua command the sun and the moon to stand still in the middle of the sky in order to give him time to complete the defeat of a small troop which was already exterminated? Why did he tell the moon to stand still at midday? How could the sun and moon remain in the same place for a day? Which commentator shall I consult for an explanation of this extraordinary truth?

32°. What shall I say of Jephthah immolating his daughter, and having forty-two thousand Jews of the tribe of Ephraim, who could not say *Shibboleth*, put to death?

33°. Ought I to admit or deny that the Jewish law nowhere speaks of punishment or reward after death? How is it that neither Moses nor Joshua ever spoke of the immortality of the soul, a dogma well known to the ancient Egyptians, Chaldæans, Persians, and Greeks, but hardly known to the Jews until after the time of Alexander, and always rejected by the Sadducees because it is not in the Pentateuch?

34°. What gloss must I put on the story of the Levite who, coming on his ass to the Benjamite town Gibeah, excited the passion of all the Gibeonites? He abandoned his wife to them, and she died the next day.

35°. I need your advice to enable me to understand the nineteenth verse of the first chapter of Judges: "And the Lord was with Judah: and he drave out the inhabitants of the mountain: but could not drive out the inhabitants of the valley, because they had chariots of iron." I cannot, of my own feeble lights, understand how the God of heaven and earth, who had so often superseded the order of nature and suspended the eternal laws in favour of the Jewish people, was unable to vanquish the inhabitants of a valley because they had iron chariots. Can it be true that, as some learned men say, the Jews at that time regarded their God as a local and protecting deity, sometimes more powerful, at other times less powerful,

than the gods of the enemy? And is this not proved
by the reply of Jephthah : " Ye possess by right what
your god Camos has given you : suffer then that we
take what our god Adonai has promised us " ?

36°. I may add that it is difficult to believe that
there were so many chariots armed with scythes in a
mountainous district, in which, as the Scriptures
often show, the height of magnificence was to be
mounted on an ass.[1]

37°. The story of Ehud gives me even greater
trouble. I see that the Jews were always in bondage,
in spite of the help of their God, who had sworn to
give them all the country between the Nile, the sea,
and the Euphrates. For eighteen years they were
subject to a petty king named Eglon, when God raised
up for them Ehud, son of Gera, who used his left hand
as well as the right. Ehud, son of Gera, made a two-
edged sword, and hid it under his cloak—as Jacques
Clément and Ravaillac did afterwards. He asks a
private audience of the king, saying that he has a
secret of the utmost importance to communicate to
him from God. Eglon respectfully rises, and Ehud
drives his sword into his belly with his left hand.
God entirely approved this deed; but, judged by the
moral code of all nations, it seems rather questionable.
Please tell me which was the most divine assassination,
that of St. Ehud, or that of St. David (who had Uriah,
the husband of his mistress, slain), or that of the
blessed Solomon, who, having seven hundred wives
and three hundred concubines, assassinated his
brother Adonias because he asked for one of them?
etc., etc., etc., etc.

38°. I pray you tell me by what trick Samson
caught three hundred foxes, tied them together by

[1] Had Voltaire known what the modern archæologist has
discovered, he would have added that the age of iron did not
even dawn until some centuries after this supposed episode;
and iron was not used in the East until about six centuries
afterwards.—J. M.

their tails, and fastened lighted torches to their hind quarters, in order to set fire to the harvests of the Philistines. Foxes are found only in wooded country. There was no forest in this district, and it seems rather difficult to catch three hundred foxes alive and tie them together by their tails. It is then said that he killed a thousand Philistines with the jaw of an ass, and that a spring issued from one of the teeth of this jaw. When it comes to the jaws of asses, you certainly owe me explanations.

39°. I also ask you for information about that good man Tobias, who slept with his eyes open, and was blinded by the droppings of a swallow; about the angel who came down expressly from what is called the empyrean to seek, with Tobias junior, the money which the Jew Gabel owed to Tobias senior; about the wife of Tobias junior, who had had seven husbands whose necks had been wrung by the devil; and about the way to restore sight to the blind with the gall of a fish. These stories are curious, and nothing is more worthy of attention—after Spanish novels; the only things to which they may be compared are the stories of Judith and Esther. But how am I to interpret the sacred text which says that the beautiful Judith descended from Simeon, son of Reuben, whereas Simeon was the brother of Reuben, according to the same sacred text, which cannot lie?

I am very fond of Esther, and think the alleged King Assuerus acted very sensibly in marrying a Jewess and living with her for six months without knowing who she was. As all the rest of the story is of much the same character, I must ask you kindly to come to my assistance, my wise masters.

40°. I need your help in regard to the history of the kings, at least as much as in regard to the history of the judges, of Tobias and his dog, of Esther, of Judith, of Ruth, etc., etc. When Saul was appointed king, the Jews were in bondage to the Philistines. Their conquerors did not allow them to have swords or lances; they were even compelled to go to the Philistines to have their ploughshares and axes sharpened. Nevertheless, Saul gives battle to the Philistines and defeats them; and in this battle he is at the head of three hundred and thirty thousand soldiers, in a little country that cannot sustain thirty thousand souls. The Jews had not at that time more than a third of Palestine, at the most, and so sterile a country does not sustain twenty thousand inhabitants to-day. The surplus population was compelled to go and earn its living by prostitution at Damascus, Tyre, and Babylon.

41°. I know not how I can justify the conduct of Samuel in cutting into pieces Agag, whom Saul had taken prisoner and put to ransom. I wonder whether our king Philip, if he captured a Moorish king, and made an agreement with him, would be approved if he cut the captured king in pieces.

42°. We owe great respect to David, who was a man after God's heart; but I fear I am not learned enough to justify, by ordinary laws, the conduct of David in associating with four hundred men of evil ways, and burdened with debt, as the Scripture says; in going to sack the house of the king's servant Nabal, and marrying his widow a week later; in offering his services to Achish, the king's enemy, and spreading fire and blood over the land of the allies of Achish, without sparing either age or sex; in taking new concubines as soon as he is on the throne; and, not content with these concubines, in stealing Bathsheba from her husband, whom he not only dishonours, but slays. I find it difficult to imagine how God could afterwards descend, in Judæa, from this adulterous and homicidal woman, who is counted among the ancestresses of the Eternal. I have already warned you that this article causes much trouble to pious souls.

43°. The wealth of David and Solomon, which amounted to more than five hundred thousand million gold ducats, seems to be not easily reconciled with the poverty of the country and with the condition to which the Jews were reduced under Saul, when they had not the means of sharpening their ploughshares and axes. Our cavalry officers will shrug their shoulders when I tell them that Solomon had four hundred thousand horses in a little country where there never were, and are not to-day, anything but asses, as I have already had the honour to represent to you.

44°. If I were to run over the history of the frightful cruelties of nearly all the kings of Judah and Israel, I fear I should scandalise, rather than edify, the weak. These kings assassinate each other a little too frequently. It is bad politics, if I am not mistaken.

45°. I see this small people almost always in bondage to the Phœnicians, Babylonians, Persians, Syrians, or Romans; and I may have some trouble in reconciling so much misery with the magnificent promises of their prophets.

46°. I know that all the eastern nations had prophets, but I do not quite understand those of the Jews. What is the meaning of the vision of Ezekiel, son of Buzi, near the river Chebar; of the four animals which had four faces and four wings each, with the feet of calves; of the wheel that had four faces; and of the firmament above the heads of the animals? How can we explain the order given by God to Ezekiel to eat a parchment book, to have himself bound, and to lie on his left side for three hundred and ninety days, and on his right side for forty days?

47°. It will be my duty to explain the great prophecy of Isaiah in regard to our Lord Jesus Christ. It is, as you know, in the seventh chapter. Rezin, king of Syria, and Pekah, kinglet of Israel, were besieging Jerusalem. Ahaz, kinglet of Jerusalem, consults the prophet Isaiah as to the issue of the siege. Isaiah replies: "God shall give you a sign: a girl (or woman) shall conceive and bear a son, and shall call his name Immanuel. Butter and honey shall he eat, that he may know to refuse the evil and choose the good. For before the child shall be able to refuse the evil and choose the good the land shall be delivered of both the kings, . . . and the Lord shall hiss for the fly that is in the uttermost part of the rivers of Egypt, and for the bee that is in the land of Assyria."

Then, in the eighth chapter, the prophet, to ensure the fulfilment of the prophecy, lies with the prophetess. She bore a son, and the Lord said to Isaiah : " Call his name Maher-shalal-hash-baz [Hasten-to-sieze-the-spoil, or Run-quickly-to-the-booty]. For before the child shall have knowledge to cry, My father and my mother, the power of Damascus shall be overthrown." I cannot plainly interpret this prophecy without your assistance.

48°. How must I understand the story of Jonah, who was sent to Nineveh to preach penance? Nineveh was not Israelitic, and it seems that Jonah was to instruct it in the Jewish law before bringing it to repent. Instead of obeying the Lord, Jonah flies to Tarshish. A storm arises, and the sailors throw Jonah into the sea to appease the tempest. God sends a great fish to swallow Jonah, and he remains three days and three nights in the belly of the fish. God orders the fish to give up Jonah, and it obeys. Jonah disembarks on the coast at Joppa. God commands him to go and tell Nineveh that in forty days it will be overturned, unless it does penance. It is more than four hundred miles from Joppa to Nineveh. Do not all the stories demand a superior knowledge which I lack? I greatly wish to confound the learned men who assert that this legend is taken from the legend of the ancient Hercules.

49°. Show me how to interpret the first verses of the prophet Hosea. God explicitly enjoins him to take a harlot and have children by her. The prophet obeys punctually. He pays his respects to Dona Gomer, daughter of Dom Diblaim, keeps her three years, and has three children—which is a model.

Then God desires another model. He orders him to lie with another gay lady, a married woman, who has already deceived her husband. The good Hosea, always obedient, has no trouble in finding a handsome lady of this character, and it costs him only fifteen pieces of silver and a measure of barley. I beg you to tell me how much the piece of silver was worth among the Jews.

50°. I have still greater need of your wise guidance in regard to the New Testament. I hardly know what to say when I have to reconcile the two genealogies of Jesus. I shall be reminded that Matthew makes Jacob the father of Joseph, while Luke makes him the son of Heli, and that this is impossible unless we change *He* into *Ja* and *li* into *cob*. I shall be asked why the one counts fifty-six generations and the other only forty-two, and why the generations are quite different; and then why only forty-one are given instead of the promised forty-two; and lastly why the genealogical tree of Joseph was given at all, seeing that he was not the father of Jesus. I fear to make a fool of myself, as so many of my predecessors have done. I trust that you will extricate me from this labyrinth.

51°. If I declare that, as Luke says, Augustus had ordered a census to be taken of the whole earth when Mary was pregnant, and that Cyrenius or Quirinus, the governor of Syria, published the decree, and that Joseph and Mary went to Bethlehem to be enumerated; and if people laugh at me, and antiquarians teach me that there never was a census of the Roman Empire, that Quintilius Varus, not Cyrenius, was at that time governor of Syria, and that Cyrenius only governed Syria ten years after the birth of Jesus, I shall be very much embarrassed, and no doubt you will extricate me from this little difficulty. For how could a book be inspired if there were one single untruth in it?

52°. When I teach that, as Matthew says, the family went into Egypt, I shall be told that that is not true, but that, as the other evangelists say, the family remained in Judæa; and if I then grant that they remained in Judæa, I shall be told that they were in Egypt. Is it not simpler to say that one can be in two places at once, as happened to St. Francis Xavier and several other saints?

53°. Astronomers may laugh at the star which led the three kings to a stable. But you are great astrologers, and will be able to explain the phenomenon. Tell me, especially, how much gold the kings presented. For you are wont to extort a good deal of it from kings and peoples. And in regard to the fourth king, Herod, why did he fear that Jesus, born in a stable, might become king of the Jews? Herod was king only by permission of the Romans; it was the business of Augustus. The massacre of the innocents is rather curious. I am disappointed that no Roman writer mentions it. An ancient and most truthful (as they all are) martyrology gives the number of these martyred infants as fourteen thousand. If you would like me to add a few thousand more, you have only to say so.

54°. You will tell me how the devil carried off God and perched him on a hill in Galilee, from which one could see all the kingdoms of the earth. The devil promising these kingdoms to God, provided God worships the devil, may scandalise many good people, whom I recommend to your notice.

55°. I beg you, when you go to a wedding feast, to tell me how God, who also went to a wedding feast, succeeded in changing water into wine for the sake of people who were already drunk.

56°. When you eat figs at breakfast towards the end of July, I beg you to tell me why God, being hungry, looked for figs at the beginning of the month of March, when it was not the season of figs.

57°. Having received your instructions on all the prodigies of this nature, I shall have to say that God was condemned to be executed for original sin. And

if I am told that there was never any question of
original sin, either in the Old or the New Testament;
that it is merely stated that Adam was condemned to
die on the day on which he should eat the fruit of
the tree of knowledge, and he did not die; and that
Augustine, bishop of Hippo, formerly a Manichæan,
was the first to set up the doctrine of original sin, I
submit to you that, as my hearers are not the simple
folk of Hippo, I run some risk of exciting derision by
speaking much without saying anything. When certain cavillers came to show me that God could not
possibly be executed because an apple was eaten four
thousand years before his death, and could not
possibly have redeemed the human race, yet, apart
from a chosen few, left the whole of it in the devil's
claws, I had only verbiage to give in reply, and went
away to hide my shame.

58°. Throw some light for me on the prophecy
which Our Lord makes in *Luke* (ch. xxi.). Jesus says
explicitly that he will come in a cloud with great
power and great glory before the generation to which
he speaks shall pass away. He did not do this; he
did not come in the clouds. If he came in some fog
or other, we know nothing about it; tell me what
you think. The apostle Paul also says to his Thessa-
lonian disciples that they will go with him in the
clouds to Jesus. Why did they not go? Does it
cost more to go to the clouds than to the third heaven?
I beg your forgiveness, but I prefer the clouds of
Aristophanes to those of Paul.

59°. Shall I say with Luke that Jesus went up to
heaven from the little village of Bethany? Shall I
state with Matthew that it was from Galilee, where
the disciples saw him for the last time? Or shall I
take the word of a learned doctor who says that
Jesus had one foot in Bethany and another in Galilee? The latter opinion seems to me the more
probable, but I will await your decision.

60°. I shall then be asked whether Peter was ever

at Rome.   I shall reply, of course, that he was pope there for twenty-five years; and the chief reason I shall give is that we have an epistle from the good man (who could neither read nor write), and that it is dated from Babylon.   There is no answer to that argument, but I should like something stronger.

61°. Please tell me why the " Apostles' Creed " was not written until the time of Jerome and Rufinus, four hundred years after the apostles.   Tell me why the earliest fathers of the Church never quote any but the gospels which we call apocryphal.   Is it not a clear proof that the four canonical gospels had not yet been written?

62°. Are you not sorry, as I am, that the early Christians forged so much bad poetry, and attributed it to the Sibyls?   And that they forged letters of Paul and Seneca, of Jesus, of Mary, and of Pilate? And that they thus set up their sect on a hundred forgeries which would be punished to-day by any court in the world?   These frauds are now recognised by all scholars. We are reduced to calling them " pious." But is it not sad that your truth should be based on lies?

63°. Tell me why, since Jesus did not institute seven sacraments, we have seven sacraments; [1] why, whereas Jesus never said that he was threefold and had two natures and two wills and one person, we make him threefold, with one person and two natures; and why, having two wills, he had not the will to instruct us in the dogmas of the Christian religion.

64°. Is the Pope infallible when he consorts with his mistress, and when he brings to supper a bottle of poisoned wine for Cardinal Cornetto? [2] When two councils anathematise each other, as has often happened, which of them is infallible?

65°. Would it not really be better to avoid these labyrinths, and simply preach virtue?   When God

---

[1] The number recognised in the Church of Rome.—J. M.

[2] The author was thinking, apparently, of Pope Alexander VI.   [Note by Voltaire.]

comes to judge us, I doubt very much if he will ask us whether grace is versatile or concomitant, whether marriage is the visible sign of an invisible thing, whether we believe that there are ten choirs of angels or nine, whether the Pope is above the council or the council above the Pope. Will it be a crime in his eyes to have prayed to him in Spanish when one does not know Latin? Shall we be visited with his cruel wrath for having eaten a pennyworth of bad meat on a certain day? And shall we be eternally rewarded if, like you, my learned masters, we ate a hundred piastres' worth of turbot, sole, and sturgeon? You do not believe it in the depth of your hearts; you believe that God will judge you by your works, not by the opinions of Thomas and Bonaventure.

Shall I not render a service to men in speaking to them only of morality? This morality is so pure, so holy, so universal, so clear, so ancient, that it seems to come from God himself, like the light which we regard as the first of his works. Has he not given men self-love to secure their preservation; benevolence, beneficence, and virtue to control their self-love; the natural need to form a society; pleasure to enjoy, pain to warn us to enjoy in moderation, passions to spur us to great deeds, and wisdom to curb our passions? Will you allow me to announce these truths to the noble people of Spain?

66°. If you bid me conceal these truths, and strictly enjoin me to announce the miracles of St. James of Galicia, or of Our Lady of Atocha, or of Maria d'Agreda (who in her ecstasies behaved in a most improper manner), tell me what I must do with those who dare to doubt? Must I, for their edification, have the ordinary and extraordinary question put to them?[1]

I await the honour of your reply

DOMINICO ZAPATA,
y verdadero, y honrado,
y caricativo.

[1] The tortures of the Inquisition.—J. M.

Zapata, receiving no answer, took to preaching God in all simplicity. He announced to men the common father, the rewarder, punisher, and pardoner. He extricated the truth from the lies, and separated religion from fanaticism; he taught and practised virtue. He was gentle, kindly, and modest; and he was burned at Valladolid in the year of grace 1631. Pray God for the soul of Brother Zapata.

EPISTLE TO THE ROMANS

(Translated from the Italian of COUNT DE CORBERA)

ARTICLE I

ILLUSTRIOUS Romans, it is not the apostle Paul who has the honour of addressing you. It is not that worthy Jew who was born at Tarsus, according to the *Acts of the Apostles,* and at Giscala according to Jerome and other fathers; a dispute that has led some to believe that one may be born in two different places at the same time, just as there are among you certain bodies which are created by a few Latin words, and are found in a hundred thousand places at the same time.[1]

It is not the bald, hot-headed man, with long and broad nose, black eyebrows, thick and continuous, and broad shoulders and crooked legs,[2] who, having carried off the daughter of his master Gamaliel, and being subsequently dissatisfied with her, divorced her;[3] and, in pique, if we may believe contemporary Jewish writers, put himself at the head of the nascent body of the Christians.

It is not that St. Paul who, when he was a servant of Gamaliel, had the good Stephen, the patron of deacons and of those who are stoned, slain with

---

[1] A shaft at the Catholic doctrine of transubstantiation.—J. M.

[2] See the *Acts of St. Thecla*, written in the first century by a disciple of St. Paul, and recognised as authentic by Tertullian, St. Cyprian, St. Gregory of Nazianzum, St. Ambrose, etc.

[3] Spurious *Acts of the Apostles*, xxi.

stones, and who, while it was done, took care of the cloaks of the murderers—a fitting employment for a priest's valet. It is not he who fell from his horse, blinded in midday by a heavenly light, and to whom God said in the air, as he says every day to so many others : " Why persecutest thou me? " It is not he who wrote to the half-Jewish, half-Christian shop-keepers of Corinth : " Have we not power to eat and to drink . . . and to lead about a sister or a wife? Who goeth to war any time at his own charge? " [1] By those fine words the Reverend Father Menou, Jesuit and apostle of Lorraine, profited so well that they brought him, at Nancy, eighty thousand francs a year, a palace, and more than one handsome woman.

It is not he who wrote to the little flock in Thessalonica that the universe was about to be destroyed, and on that account it was not worth while keeping money about one. As Paul said : " For the Lord himself shall descend from heaven with a shout, with the voice of the archangel, and with the trump of God ; and the dead in Christ shall rise first ; then we which are alive and remain shall be caught up together with them." [2]

Observe, generous Romans, that St. Paul did but announce these pleasant things to the tailors and grocers of Thessalonica in virtue of the express prophecy of Luke (ch. xxi.), who had publicly—that is, to some fifteen or sixteen chosen souls among the people—averred that this generation would not pass away before the son of man came on the clouds with great power and glory. It is true, O Romans, that Jesus came not on the clouds with a great power; but at least the popes have had this great power, and thus are the prophecies fulfilled.

He who writes this epistle to the Romans is, again, not that St. Paul, half Jew, half Christian, who,

---

[1] I *Corinthians* ix. 4, 5, and 7.
[2] I *Thessalonians* iv. 16 and 17.

having preached Jesus and announced the destruction of the Mosaic law, not only went to Judaise in
the temple of Hershalaim, which the vulgar call
Jerusalem, but, on the advice of his friend James,
observed there certain rigorous practices which the
Holy Inquisition now punishes with death.[1]

He who writes to you has been neither priest's
valet, nor murderer, nor keeper of cloaks, nor apostate, nor maker of tents, nor buried in the depths of
the sea, like Jonah, for twenty-four hours, nor caught
up to the third heaven, like Elias, without learning
what the third heaven is.

He who writes to you is more a citizen than this
Saul Paul, who, it is said, boasted of being one, and
assuredly was not. For Tarsus, if he came from
there, was not made a Roman colony until the time
of Caracalla [A.D. 211–217]; and Giscala in Galilee,
from which it is more probable that he came, since
he was of the tribe of Benjamin, was certainly not a
Roman town. Roman citizenship was not bestowed
on Jews at Tarsus or anywhere else. The author of
the *Acts of the Apostles* (xvi. 37) asserts that this Jew
Paul and another Jew named Silas were arrested by
the authorities in the town of Philippi in Macedonia
(a town founded by the father of Alexander, near
which the battle between Cassius and Brutus, on the
one side, and Antony and Octavian, on the other,
decided the fate of your empire). Paul and Silas
were scourged for stirring up the populace, and Paul
said to the officers : " They have beaten us, being
Romans " (*Acts* xvi. 37). Commentators freely
admit that Silas was not a Roman citizen. They do
not say that the author of *Acts* lied, but they agree
that what he says is untrue; and I am sorry for the
Holy Spirit, who, no doubt, dictated the *Acts of the
Apostles*.

In fine, he who now writes to the descendants of
Marcellus, the Scipios, the Catos, Cicero, Titus, and

[1] *Acts* xxi.

the Antonines, is a Roman gentleman of an ancient and transplanted family, one who cherishes his venerable country, bemoans her condition, and has left his heart in her Capitol.

Romans, listen to your fellow citizen; listen to Rome and your ancient valour.

L'Italico valor non è ancor morto.

ARTICLE II

When I travelled among you, I wept to see the Zocolanti occupying that very Capitol to which Paulus Emilius led king Perseus, the descendant of Alexander, chained to his triumphal car; that temple to which the Scipios had brought the spoils of Carthage, and in which Pompey triumphed over Asia, Africa, and Europe. But even more bitter were my tears when I recalled the feast that Cæsar spread for our ancestors on twenty-two thousand tables, and when I compared the *congiaria*, that immense free distribution of corn, with the scanty and poor bread that you eat to-day, sold to you at so high a price by the apostolic chamber. Alas! you cannot even sow your soil without the permission of these apostles; and, indeed, what have you with which to sow it? There is not a citizen among you, save a few that live in the Trastevere quarter, who has a plough. Your God fed five thousand men, to say nothing of the women and children, with five loaves and two gudgeons, according to St. John; four thousand men, according to Matthew.[1] You, Romans, are made to swallow the gudgeon [2] without receiving

---

[1] Matthew gives five thousand men and five loaves in chapter xiv., and four thousand men and five loaves in chapter xv. Apparently, they are two different miracles, which makes in all nine thousand men and at least nine thousand women. If you add nine thousand children, the total number of diners amounts to twenty-seven thousand—which is considerable.

[2] A pun of which the point is lost in English. The French phrase, to make a man " swallow the gudgeon," means to

any bread. The successors of Lucullus are reduced to the holy practice of fasting.

Your climate has never changed, whatever be said to the contrary. Who, then, has so greatly changed your soil, your fortunes, and your spirit? Whence comes it that the whole country from the gates of Rome to Ostia is inhabited only by reptiles? Why do we find that, from Montefiascone to Viterbo, and in the whole region through which the Appian Way still leads to Naples, a vast desert has replaced the smiling land that was once covered with palaces, gardens, harvests, and countless numbers of citizens? I sought the Forum Romanum of Trajan, that square once paved with reticulated marble, surrounded by a colonnaded peristyle and adorned with a hundred statues; and what I found was the Campo Vacino, the cattle-market, a market of lean and milkless cows. And I asked myself: Where are those two million Romans who once peopled this capital? I found that on the average only 3,500 children are now born annually in Rome. Setting aside Jews, priests, and foreigners, Rome cannot have one hundred thousand inhabitants. I asked of them: Whose is this splendid building that I see, girt about with ruins? It belongs to the monks, they said. Here once was the house of Augustus; there Cicero dwelt, and there Pompey. On their ruins have arisen convents.

I wept, Romans; and I think highly enough of you to believe that you weep with me.

ARTICLE III

It was explained to me that an aged priest, who has been appointed Pope by other priests, cannot find either the time or the will to relieve your misery. He can think only of living. What interest should

---

" gull " a man. Voltaire turns the " two little fishes " of the gospel into gudgeons to accommodate his joke.—J. M.

he take in Romans? He is himself rarely a Roman.
What care should he take of an estate that will not
pass to his children? Rome is not his patrimony, as
it was that of the Cæsars. It is an ecclesiastical
benefice; the papacy is a kind of commendatory
abbey,[1] which each abbot ruins while he lives. The
Cæsars had a real interest in seeing Rome flourish;
the patricians, under the Republic, had an even
greater interest. No dignities could be obtained
unless the people were won with benefits, cajoled by
the appearance of virtue, or fired by great victories.
A pope shuts himself up with his money and his
unleavened bread, and gives only his blessing to the
people that was once known as " the People King."

Your misfortunes began with the transfer of the
empire of Rome to the bounds of Thrace. Constantine, chosen emperor by a few barbaric cohorts in
distant England, triumphed over the Maxentius
chosen by you. Maxentius was drowned in the Tiber
in the rout, and left the Empire to his rival. But
the conqueror went to hide himself on the shores of
the Black Sea; he could not have done more if he
had been beaten. Stained with debauch and crime,
murderer of his father-in-law, brother-in-law, nephew,
son, and wife, abhorred by the Romans, he abandoned the ancient religion under which they had con-
quered so many States, and cast himself into the
arms of the Christians who had found the money to
which he owed his crown.[2] He thus betrayed the

---

[1] In France, an abbey of which the " abbot " was a kind
of absentee landlord. He lived at Paris, with the title and
revenue, and left the work to a sub-abbot.—J. M.

[2] The indictment is too severe. The later years of Constantine were marked by silly extravagance, but not debauch.
The execution of his father-in-law was justified. His (partial)
acceptance of Christianity was earlier than Voltaire supposes,
and there is no serious ground for suggesting large payments
of money. But it is now beyond question that he put his
brother-in-law (Licinius) to death treacherously, had his wife,
son, and nephew murdered, and greatly degenerated in later
life.—J. M.

Empire as soon as he obtained it, and, in transplanting to the Bosphorus the great tree that had sheltered Europe, Africa, and Asia Minor, he did fatal injury to its roots.

Your next misfortune was this ecclesiastical maxim, quoted in a celebrated French poem, " Le Lutrin," and very gravely true : " Ruin the world, if need be; it is the spirit of the Church." The Church fought the ancient religion of the Empire, and tore its own entrails in the struggle, dividing, with equal fury and imprudence, on a hundred incomprehensible questions of which none had ever heard before. The Christian sects, hounding each other with fire and sword for metaphysical chimæras and sophisms of the school, united to seize the spoils of the priesthood founded by Numa. They did not rest until they had destroyed the altar of Victory at Rome.

St. Ambrose, passing from the bar to the bishopric of Milan without being a deacon, and your Damasus, whom a schism made Bishop of Rome, profited by this fatal success. They secured the destruction of the altar of Victory, which had been set up on the Capitol [1] nearly eight hundred years before—a monument of the courage of your ancestors, destined to maintain their valour in their descendants. The emblematic figure of Victory was no object of idolatry, like your statues of Antony of Padua (who " hears those whom God will not hear "), of Francis of Assisi (who is represented over the door of a church at Rheims with this inscription : " To Francis and Jesus, both crucified "), of St. Crepin, St. Barbe, and so many others; or like the blood of a score of saints (headed by your patron Januarius, whom the rest of the earth knows not) that is liquefied at Naples on certain days, or the prepuce and navel of Jesus, or the milk, and hair, and shift, and petticoat of his mother. These are idolatries, as disgusting as they are accredited. But this Victory, surmounting a

[1] No; in the Senate.—J. M.

globe, with outspread wings, a sword in hand, and head crowned with laurels, was merely the noble device of the Roman Empire, the symbol of virtue. Fanaticism robbed you of the pledge of your glory.

With what effrontery did these new enthusiasts dare to substitute their Rochs, and Fiacres, and Eustaces, and Ursulas, and Scholasticas for Neptune, the ruler of the seas; Mars, the god of war; and Juno, the ruler of the air, under the sovereignty of the great Zeus, the eternal Demiourgos, master of the elements, the gods, and men ! A thousand times more idolatrous than your ancestors, these maniacs bade you worship the bones of the dead. These plagiarists of antiquity borrowed the lustral water of the Romans and Greeks, their procession, the confession that was made in the mysteries of Ceres and Isis, their incense, libations, hymns, and the very garments of their priests. They spoiled the old religion, and clad themselves in its vesture. Even to-day they bow down before the statues of unknown men, while they heap reproaches on a Pericles, a Solon, a Miltiades, a Cicero, a Scipio, or a Cato for bending the knee before these emblems of divinity.

Nay, is there a single episode in the Old or the New Testament that has not been copied from the ancient mythologies of India, Chaldæa, Egypt, and Greece? Is not the sacrifice of Idomene the plain source of that of Jephtha? Is not the roe of Iphigenia the ram of Isaac? Do you not recognise Eurydice in Edith, the wife of Lot? Minerva and the winged horse Pegasus drew fountains from the rocks when they struck them; the same prodigy is ascribed to Moses. Bacchus had crossed the Red Sea dryshod before he did, and he had caused the sun and moon to stand still before Joshua. We have the same legends, the same extravagances, on every side.

There is not a single miraculous action in the Gospels that you will not find in much earlier writers.

The goat Amalthæa had a horn of plenty long before
it was said that Jesus had fed five thousand men,
not to speak of the women, with two fishes. The
daughters of Anius have changed water into wine
and oil before there was any question of the marriage-
feast of Cana.   Athalide, Hippolytus, Alcestis, Pelops,
and Heres had returned to life long before men spoke
of the resurrection of Jesus; and Romulus was born
of a vestal virgin more than seven hundred years
before Jesus began to be regarded as virgin-born.
Compare, and judge for yourselves.

ARTICLE IV

When your altar of Victory had been destroyed,
the barbarians came and finished the work of the
priests.   Rome became the prey and the sport of
nations that it had so long ruled, if not repressed.

It is true that you still had consuls, a senate,
municipal laws; but the popes have robbed you of
what the Huns and Goths had left you.

It was in earlier times unheard of that a priest
should set up royal rights in any city of the Empire.
It is well known all over Europe, except in your
chancellory, that, until the time of Gregory VII., your
pope was but a metropolitan bishop, subject to the
Greek, then the Frankish, emperors, and then to the
house of Saxony; receiving investiture from them,
compelled to send a profession of faith to the bishops
of Ravenna and Milan, as we read expressly in your
Diarium Romanum.   His title of " patriarch of the
west " gave him much prestige, but no sovereign
rights.   A priest-king was a blasphemy in a religion
of which the founder expressly says in the gospels :
" There shall be no first and last among you."
Weigh well, Romans, these other words that are put
in the mouth of Jesus : " To sit on my right hand
and on my left it is not mine to give, but for whom

it is prepared of my father." [1] Know, moreover, that the Jews meant, and still mean, by " son of God " a just man. Inquire of the eight thousand Jews who sell old clothes, as they ever have done, in your city, and pay close attention to the following words : " Whosoever will be great among you, let him be your minister. The Son of Man came not to be ministered unto, but to minister." [2]

Do these clear and precise words mean that Boniface VIII. was bound to crush the Colonna family; that Alexander VI. was bound to poison so many Roman barons; or that the bishop of Rome received from God, in a time of anarchy, the duchy of Rome, Ferrara, Bologna, the March of Ancona, Castro, and Ronciglione, and all the country from Viterbo to Terracina, which have been wrested from their lawful owners? Think you, Romans, that Jesus was sent on earth by God solely for the Rezzonico?

ARTICLE V

You will ask me by what means this strange revolution of all divine and human laws was brought about. I am about to tell you; and I defy the most zealous fanatic in whom there is still a spark of reason, and the most determined rogue who has still a trace of decency in his soul, to resist the force of the truth, if he reads this important inquiry with the attention it deserves.

It is certain and undoubted that the earliest societies of the Galilæans, afterwards called Christians, remained in obscurity, in the mud of the cities; and it is certain that, when these Christians began to write, they entrusted their books only to those who had been initiated into their mysteries. They were not even given to the catechumens, much less to partisans of the imperial religion. No Roman

---

[1] *Matthew* xx. 23.
[2] *Matthew* xx. 26 and 27.

before the time of Trajan [A.D. 98–117] knew that the gospels existed; no Greek or Latin writer has ever quoted the word "gospel"; Plutarch, Lucian, Petronius, and Apuleius, who speak of everything, are entirely ignorant of the existence of gospels. This proof, with a hundred others, shows the absurdity of those authors who now hold, or pretend to hold, that the disciples of Jesus died for the truth of these gospels, of which the Romans did not hear a word during two hundred years. The half-Jew, half-Christian Galilæans, separated from the disciples of John, and from the Therapeuts, Essenians, Judaites, Herodians, Sadducees, and Pharisees, recruited their little flock among the lowest of the people, not, indeed, by means of books, but of speech, by catechising the women and girls (*Acts* xvi. 13 and 14) and children, and passing from town to town; in a word, like all other sects.

Tell me frankly, Romans, what your ancestors would have said if St. Paul, or Simon Barjona, or Matthias, or Matthew, or Luke, had appeared in the Senate and said : " Our God, Jesus, who passed as the son of a carpenter during life, was born in the year 752 from the foundation of Rome, under the governorship of Cyrenius (*Luke* ii. 2), in a Jewish village called Bethlehem, to which his father Joseph and his mother Mariah had gone to be included in the census which Augustus had ordered. This God was born in a stable, between an ox and an ass.[1] The angels came down from heaven and informed the peasants of his birth; a new star appeared in the heavens, and led to him three kings or wise men from the east, who brought him a tribute of incense, myrrh, and gold; but in spite of this gold he was

---

[1] All Christians believe that Jesus was born in a stable, between an ox and an ass. There is, however, no mention of this in the gospels. It was imagined by Justin, and is mentioned by Lactantius, or at least the author of a bad Latin poem on the passions, which is attributed to Lactantius.

poor throughout life.   Herod, who was then dying,
and whom you had made king, having learned that
the new-born child was king of the Jews, had fourteen thousand new-born infants of the district put to
death, to make sure that the king was included
(*Matthew* ii. 16).   However, one of our writers inspired by God says that the God-king child fled to
Egypt ; and another writer, equally inspired by God,
says that the child remained at Bethlehem (*Luke* ii.
39).   One of these sacred and infallible writers
draws up a royal genealogy for him ; another com-
poses for him an entirely different royal genealogy.
Jesus preaches to the peasants, and turns water into
wine for them at a marriage feast.   Jesus is taken by
the devil up into a mountain.   He drives out devils,
and sends them into the body of two thousand pigs
in Galilee, where there never were any pigs.   He
greatly insulted the magistrates, and the prætor
Pontius had him executed.   When he had been
executed, he manifested his divinity.   The earth
trembled ; the dead left their graves, and walked
about in the city before the eyes of Pontius.   There
was an eclipse of the sun at midday, at a time of full
moon, although that is impossible   He rose again
secretly, went up to heaven, and sent down another
god, who fell on the heads of his disciples in tongues
of fire.   May these same tongues fall on your heads,
conscript fathers ; become Christians.''
      If the lowest official in the Senate had condescended
to answer this discourse, he would have said : '' You
are weak-minded rogues, and ought to be put in the
asylum for the insane.   You lie when you say that
your God was born in the year of Rome 752, under
the governorship of Cyrenius, the proconsul of Syria.
Cyrenius did not govern Syria until more than ten
years afterwards, as our registers prove.   Quintilius
Varus was at that time proconsul of Syria.
      '' You lie when you say that Augustus ordered a
census of ' all the world.'   You must be very ignorant

not to know that Augustus was master only of one-tenth of the world. If by ' all the world ' you mean the Roman Empire, know that neither Augustus nor anybody else ever undertook such a census. Know that there was but one single enumeration of the citizens of Rome and its territory under Augustus, and that the number amounted to four million citizens; and unless your carpenter Joseph and his wife Mariah brought forth your God in a suburb of Rome, and this Jewish carpenter was a Roman citizen, he cannot possibly have been included.

" You are telling a ridiculous untruth with your three kings and new star, and the little massacred children, and the dead rising again and walking in the streets under the eyes of Pontius Pilate, who never wrote us a word about it, etc., etc.

" You are lying when you speak of an eclipse of the sun at a time of full moon. Our prætor Pontius Pilate would have written to us about it, and we, together with all the nations of the earth, would have witnessed this eclipse. Return to your work, you fanatical peasants, and thank the Senate that it has too much disdain to punish you."

ARTICLE VI

It is clear that the first half-Jewish Christians took care not to address themselves to the Roman Senators, nor to any man of position or anyone above the lowest level of the people. It is well known that they appealed only to the lowest class. To these they boasted of healing nervous diseases, epilepsy, and uterine convulsions, which ignorant folk, among the Romans as well as among the Jews, Egyptians, Greeks, and Syrians, regarded as the work of charms or diabolical possession. There must assuredly have been some cases of healing. Some were cured in the name of Esculapius, and we have since discovered at Rome a monument of a miracle of Esculapius, with the names of the witnesses. Others were healed in the name of Isis, or of the Syrian goddess; others in the name of Jesus, etc. The common people healed in one of these names believed in those who propagated it.

ARTICLE VII

Thus the Christians made progress among the people by a device that invariably seduces ignorant folk. But they had a still more powerful means. They declaimed against the rich. They preached community of goods; in their secret meetings they enjoined their neophytes to give them the little money they had earned; and they quoted the alleged instance of Sapphira and Ananias (*Acts* v. 1–11), whom Simon Barjona, called Cephas, which means Peter, caused to die suddenly because they had kept a crown to themselves—the first and most detestable example of priestly covetousness.

But they would not have succeeded in extorting the money of their neophytes if they had not preached the doctrine of the cynic philosophers—the idea of voluntary poverty. Even this, however, was not enough to form a new flock. The end of the world had been long announced. You will find it in Epicurus and Lucretius, his chief disciple. Ovid had said, in the days of Augustus :—

> Esse quoque in fatis meminisceret adfore tempus,
> Quo mare, quo tellus, correptaque regio coeli
> Ardeat, et mundi moles operosa laboret.[1]

According to others, the world had been made by a fortuitous concourse of atoms, and would be destroyed by another fortuitous concourse, as we find in the poems of Lucretius.

---

[1] A time by fate appointed was to come,
When sea, and earth, and all the realm of heaven
Should flame, and ruin seize the world's great mass.—J. M.

This idea came originally from the Brahmans of India. Many Jews had adopted it by the time of Herod. It is formally stated in the gospel of Luke, as you have seen; it is in Paul's epistles; and it is in all those who are known as fathers of the Church. The world was about to be destroyed, it was thought; and the Christians announced a new Jerusalem, which was seen in the air by night.[1] The Jews talked of nothing but a new kingdom of heaven; it was the system of John the Baptist, who had introduced on the Jordan the ancient Hindoo practice of baptism in the Ganges. Baptism was practised by the Egyptians, and adopted by the Jews. This new kingdom of heaven, to which the poor alone would be admitted, was preached by Jesus and his followers. They threatened with eternal torment those who would not believe in the new heaven. This hell, invented by the first Zoroaster, became one of the chief points of Egyptian theology.[2] From the latter came the barque of Charon, Cerberus, the river Lethe, Tartarus, and the Furies. From Egypt the idea passed to Greece, and from there to the Romans; the Jews were unacquainted with it until the time when the Pharisees preached it, shortly before the reign of Herod. It was one of their contradictions to admit both hell and metempsychosis (trans-migration of souls); but who would look for reason-ing among the Jews? Their powers in that direction are confined to money matters. The Sadducees and Samaritans rejected the immortality of the soul, because it is not found anywhere in the Mosaic law.

This was the great spring which the early Christians, all half-Jewish, relied upon to put the new machinery in action: community of goods, secret

---

[1] See *Revelation*, Justin, and Tertullian.

[2] In Voltaire's time, naturally, the relative priority of Indian, Egyptian, Babylonian, and Persian civilisations was quite unknown, and his idea of their relations to each other cannot hold to-day.—J. M.

meals, hidden mysteries, gospels read to the initiated only, paradise for the poor, hell for the rich, and exorcisms by charlatans. Here, in strict truth, we have the first foundations of the Christian sect. If I deceive you—or, rather, if I deliberately deceive you—I pray the God of the universe, the God of all men, to wither the hand that writes this, to shatter with his lightning a head that is convinced of the existence of a good and just God, and to tear out from me a heart that worships him.

ARTICLE VIII

Let us now, Romans, consider the artifices, roguery, and forgery to which the Christians themselves have given the name of "pious frauds"; frauds that have cost you your liberty and your goods, and have brought down the conquerors of Europe to a most lamentable slavery. I again take God to witness that I will say no word that is not amply proved. If I wished to use all the arms of reason against fanaticism, all the piercing darts of truth against error, I should speak to you first of that prodigious number of contradictory gospels which your popes themselves now recognise to be false. They show, at least, that there were forgers among the first Christians. This, however, is very well known. I have to tell you of impostures that are not generally known, and are a thousand times more pernicious.

First Imposture

It is a very ancient superstition that the last words of the dying are prophetic, or are, at least, sacred maxims and venerable precepts. It was believed that the soul, about to dissolve the union with the body and already half united to the Deity, had a cloudless vision of the future and of truth. Following this prejudice, the Judæo-Christians forge, in the first century of the Church, the *Testament of the Twelve Patriarchs,* written in Greek, to serve as a prediction or a preparation for the new kingdom of Jesus. In the testament of Reuben we find these words : " Adore his seed, for he will die for you, in wars visible and invisible, and he will be your king for ever." This prophecy is applied to Jesus, in the usual way of those who wrote fifty-four gospels in various places, and who nearly all endeavoured to find in Jewish writers, especially those who were called prophets, passages that could be twisted in favour of Jesus. They even added some that are clearly recognised as false. The author of the " Testament of the Patriarchs " is one of the most impudent and clumsy forgers that ever spoiled good parchment. His book was written in Alexandria, in the school of a certain Mark.

Second Chief Imposture

They forged letters from the king of Edessa to Jesus, and from Jesus to this supposed prince. There was no king at Edessa, which was a town under the Syrian governor ; the petty prince of Edessa never had the title of king. Moreover, it is not said in any of the gospels that Jesus could write ; and if he could, he would have left some proof of it to his disciples. Hence these letters are now declared by all scholars to be forgeries.

Third Chief Imposture

(which contains several)

They forged *Acts of Pilate,* letters of Pilate, and even a history of Pilate's wife. The letters of Pilate are especially interesting. Here is a fragment of one :—

" It happened a short time ago, and I have verified it, that the Jews in their envy drew on themselves a cruel condemnation. Their God having promised that he would send his holy one to them from heaven to be their legitimate king, and that he should be born of a virgin, did indeed send him when I was procurator in Judæa. The leaders of the Jews denounced him to me as a magician. I believed it, and had him scourged, and handed him over to them; and they crucified him. They put guards about his tomb, but he rose again the third day."

To this forgery I may add that of the rescript of Tiberius to the Senate, to raise Jesus to the rank of the Imperial gods, and the ridiculous letters of the philosopher Seneca to Paul, and of Paul to Seneca, written in barbaric Latin; also the letters of the Virgin Mary to St. Ignatius, and many other clumsy fictions of the same nature. I will not draw out this list of impostures. It would amaze you if I enumerated them one by one.

Fourth Imposture

The boldest, perhaps, and clumsiest of these forgeries is that of the prophecies attributed to the Sibyls, foretelling the incarnation, miracles, and death of Jesus, in acrostic verse. This piece of folly, unknown to the Romans, fed the belief of the catechumens. It circulated among us for eight centuries, and we still sing in one of our hymns [1] " teste David cum Sibylla " [witness David and the Sibyl].

You are astonished, no doubt, that this despicable comedy was maintained so long, and that men could be led with such a bridle as that. But as the Christians were plunged in the most stupid barbarism for fifteen hundred years, as books were very rare and theologians very astute, one could say anything at all to poor wretches who would believe anything at all.

Fifth Imposture

Illustrious and unfortunate Romans, before we come to the pernicious untruths which have cost you your liberty, your property, and your glory, and put

[1] The famous " Dies irae," sung in Catholic funeral services to-day in England.—J. M.

you under the yoke of a priest; before I speak to you of the alleged pontificate of Simon Barjona, who is said to have been bishop of Rome for twenty-five years, you must be informed of the " Apostolic Constitutions," the first foundation of the hierarchy that crushes you to-day.

At the beginning of the second century there was no such thing as an *episcopos* (" overseer ") or bishop, clothed with real dignity for life, unalterably attached to a certain see, and distinguished from other men by his clothes; bishops, in fact, dressed like ordinary laymen until the middle of the fifth century. The meeting was held in a chamber of some retired house. The minister was chosen by the initiated, and continued his work as long as they were satisfied. There were no altars, candles, or incense; the earliest fathers of the Church speak of altars and temples with a shudder.[1] They were content to make a collection and sup together. When the Christian society had grown, however, ambition set up an hierarchy. How did they go about it? The rogues who led the enthusiasts made them believe that they had discovered the apostolic constitutions written by St. John and St. Matthew : " quae ego Matthæus et Joannes vobis tradidimus [which I, Matthew, and John have given you]." [2] In these Matthew is supposed to say (II. xxxvi.) : " Be ye careful not to judge your bishop, for it is given to the priests alone to judge." Matthew and John say (II. xxxiv.) : " As much as the soul is above the body, so much higher is the priesthood than royalty; consider your bishop as a king, an absolute master (*dominum*); give him your fruits, your works, your firstlings, your tithes, your savings, the first and tenth part of your wine, oil, and corn, etc." Again (II. xxx.) : " Let the bishop be a god to you, and the deacon a prophet; " and (II. xxxviii.) : " In the festivals let

[1] Justin and Tertullian.
[2] *Apostolic Constitutions*, Bk. II., ch. lvii.

the deacon have a double portion, and the priest double that of the deacon; and if they be not at table, send the portions to them."

You see, Romans, the origin of your custom of spreading your tables to give indigestion to your pontiffs. Would to God they had confined themselves to the sin of gluttony.

You will further observe with care, in regard to this imposture of the constitutions of the apostles, that it is an authentic monument of the dogmas of the second century, and that forgery at least does homage to truth in maintaining a complete silence about innovations that could not be foreseen—innovations with which you have been deluged century after century. You will find, in this second-century document, neither trinity, nor consubstantiality, nor transubstantiation, nor auricular confession. You will not find in it that the mother of Jesus was the mother of God, that Jesus had two natures and two wills, or that the Holy Ghost proceeds from the father and the son. All these singular ornaments of imagination, unknown to the religion of the gospels, have been added since to the crude structure which fanaticism and ignorance raised up in the first centuries.

You will assuredly find in it three persons, but not three persons in one God. Read with all the acuteness of your mind, the only treasure that your tyrants have left you, the common prayer which the Christians, by the mouth of their bishop, offered in their meetings in the second century :

" O all-powerful, unengendered, inaccessible God, the one true God, father of Christ thy only son, God of the paraclete, God of all, thou hast made the disciples of Christ doctors, etc." [1]

Here, clearly, is one sole God who commands Christ and the paraclete [Holy Ghost]. Judge for yourselves if that has any resemblance to the trinity and consubstantiality which were afterwards declared at

[1] *Apostolic Constitutions*, VIII. vi.

Nicæa, in spite of the strong protest of eighteen bishops and two thousand priests.[1]

In another place (III. xvi.) the author of the *Apostolic Constitutions*, who is probably a bishop of the Christians at Rome, says expressly that the father is God above all.

That is the doctrine of Paul, finding expression so frequently in his epistles. " We have peace in God through Our Lord Jesus Christ " (*Romans* v. 1). " If through the offence of one many be dead, much more the grace of God, and the gift by grace, which is by one man, Jesus Christ, hath abounded unto many " (*Romans* v. 15). " We are heirs of God, and joint-heirs with Christ " (*Romans* viii. 17). " Receive ye one another, as Christ also received us to the glory of God " (*Romans* xv. 7). " To God only wise, be glory through Jesus Christ for ever " (*Romans* xvi. 27). " That the God of Our Lord Jesus Christ, the father of glory, may give unto you the spirit of wisdom " (*Ephesians* i. 17).

Thus does the Jew-Christian Saul Paul always express himself, and thus is Jesus himself made to speak in the gospels. " My father is greater than I " (*John* xiv. 28); that is to say, God can do what men cannot do. All the Jews said " my father " when they spoke of God.

The Lord's Prayer begins with the words " Our Father." Jesus said : " Of that day and hour knoweth no man, no, not the angels of heaven, but my father only " (*Matthew* xxiv. 36); and " That is not mine to give, but for whom it is prepared by my Father " (*Matthew* xx. 23). It is also very remarkable that when Jesus awaited arrest, and sweated blood and water, he cried out : " Father, remove this cup from me " (*Luke* xxii. 42). No gospel has put into his mouth the blasphemy that he was God, or consubstantial with God.

[1] See the *History of the Church of Constantinople and Alexandria*, in the Bodleian Library.

You will ask me, Romans, why and how he was made into a God in the course of time? I will ask you in turn why and how Bacchus, Perseus, Hercules, and Romulus were made gods? In their case, moreover, the sacrilege did not go so far as to give them the title of supreme god and creator. This blasphemy was reserved for the Christian outgrowth of the Jewish sect.

Sixth Chief Imposture

I pass over the countless impostures of " The Travels of Simon Barjona," the " Gospel of Simon Barjona," his " Apocalypse," the " Apocalypse " of Cerinthus (ridiculously attributed to John), the epistles of Barnaby, the " Gospel of the Twelve Apostles," their liturgies, the " Canons of the Council of the Apostles," the " Apostles' Creed," the " Travels of Matthew," the " Travels of Thomas," and so many other vagaries that are now recognised to be the work of forgers, who passed them off under venerated Christian names.

I will not insist much on the romance of the alleged Pope St. Clement, who calls himself the first successor of St. Peter. I will note only that Simon Barjona and he met an old man, who complained of the unfaithfulness of his wife, who had lain with his servant. Clement asks how he learned it. " By my wife's horoscope," said the good man, " and from my brother, with whom she wished to lie, but he would not." From these words Clement recognised his father in the old man.[1] From Peter Clement learned that he was of the blood of the Cæsars. On such romances, Romans, was the papal power set up !

Seventh Chief Imposture

(On the Supposed Pontificate of Simon Barjona, Called Peter)

Who was the first to say that Simon, the poor fisherman, came from Galilee to Rome, spoke Latin

[1] *Recognitions* of St. Clement, Bk. IX., Nos. 32–35.

there (though he could not possibly know more than his native dialect), and in the end was Pope of Rome for twenty-five years? It was a Syrian named Abdias, who lived about the end of the first century, and is said to have been Bishop of Babylon (a good bishopric). He wrote in Syriac, and we have his work in a Latin translation by Julius the African. Listen well to what this intelligent writer says. He was an eye-witness, and his testimony is irrefragable.

Simon Barjona Peter, having, he says, raised to life Tabitha, or Dorcas, the sempstress of the apostles, and having been put in prison by the orders of King Herod (though there was no King Herod at the time); and an angel having opened the doors of the prison for him (after the custom of angels), met, in Cæsarea, the other Simon, of Samaria, known as the Magician (Magus), who also performed miracles. They began to defy each other. Simon the Samaritan went off to the Emperor Nero at Rome. Simon Barjona followed him, and the Emperor received them excellently. A cousin of the Emperor had died, and it was a question which of them could restore him to life. The Samaritan has the honour of opening the ceremony. He calls upon God, and the dead man gives signs of life and shakes his head. Simon Peter calls on Jesus Christ, and tells the dead man to rise; forthwith he does rise, and embraces Peter. Then follows the well-known story of the two dogs. Then Abdias tells how Simon flew in the air, and his rival Simon Peter brought him down. Simon the Magician broke his legs, and Nero had Simon Peter crucified, head downwards, for breaking the legs of the other Simon.

This harlequinade was described, not only by Abdias, but by someone named Marcellus, and by a certain Hegesippus, whom Eusebius often quotes in his history. Pray notice, judicious Romans, how this Simon Peter may have reigned spiritually in your city for twenty-five years. He came to it under Nero, according to the earliest writers of the Church; he died under Nero; and Nero reigned only thirteen years.

Read the *Acts of the Apostles*. Is there any question therein of Peter going to Rome? Not the least mention. Do you not see that, when the fiction began that Peter was the first of the apostles, it was thought that the imperial city alone was worthy of him? See how clumsily you have been deluded in everything. Is it possible that the son of God, nay God himself, should have made use of a play on words, a ridiculous pun, to make Simon Barjona the head of his Church : " Thou art Peter, and upon this rock [petra] I will build my Church." Had Barjona been called Pumpkin, Jesus might have said to him : " Thou art Pumpkin, and Pumpkin shall henceforward be the king of the fruits in my garden." [1]

For more than three hundred years the alleged successor of a Galilean peasant was unknown to Rome. Let us now see how the popes became your masters.

Eighth Imposture

No one who is acquainted with the history of the Greek and Latin Churches can be unaware that the metropolitan sees established their chief rights at the Council of Chalcedon, convoked in the year 451 by the order of the Emperor Marcian and of Pulcheria [his wife], and composed of six hundred and thirty bishops. The Senators who presided in the Emperor's name had on their right the patriarchs of Alexandria and Jerusalem, on their left the patriarch of Constantinople and the deputies of the patriarch of Rome. It was in virtue of the canons of this Council that the episcopal sees shared the dignities of the cities in which they were situated. The bishops of the two

[1] The pun is lost to readers of the English Bible. In French, as in Syro-Chaldaic and Greek and (approximately) Latin, " Peter " and " rock " are the same word. We have it in " salt-petre."—J. M.

imperial cities, Rome and Constantinople, were declared to be the first bishops, with equal prerogatives, by the celebrated twenty-eighth canon :

" The fathers have justly granted prerogatives to the see of ancient Rome, as to a reigning city, and the 150 bishops of the first Council of Constantinople, very dear to God, have for the same reason given the same privileges to the new Rome; they have rightly thought that this city, in which the Emperor and Senate reside, should be equal to it in all ecclesiastical matters."

The popes have always contested the authenticity of this canon; they have twisted and perverted its whole meaning. What did they do at length to evade this equality and gradually to destroy all the titles of subjection which placed them under the emperors like all other men? They forged the famous donation of Constantine, which has been for many centuries so strictly regarded as genuine that it was a mortal and unpardonable sin to doubt it, and whoever did so incurred the greater excommunication by the very fact of doubting.

A very pretty thing was this donation of Constantine to Bishop Sylvester.

" We," says the Emperor, " with all our satraps and the whole Roman people, have thought it good to give to the successors of St. Peter a greater power than that of our serene majesty." Do you not think, Romans, that the word " satrap " comes in very well there?

With equal authenticity, Constantine goes on, in this noble diploma, to say that he has put the Apostles Peter and Paul in large amber caskets; that he has built the churches of St. Peter and St. Paul; that he has given them vast domains in Judæa, Greece, Thrace, Asia, etc. (to maintain the luminary); that he has given to the pope his Lateran palace, with chamberlains and guards; and that, lastly, he gives him, as a pure donation for himself and his successors, the city of Rome, Italy, and all the western provinces; and all this is given to thank the Pope Sylvester for having cured him of leprosy, and having baptised him—though, in point of fact, he was baptised only on his deathbed, by Eusebius, bishop of Nicomedia.

Never was there a document more ridiculous from one end to the other, yet more accredited in the ignorant ages in which Europe was so long detained after the fall of your empire.

Ninth Imposture

I pass over the thousand and one little daily impostures to come at once to the great fraud of the Decretals.

These false Decretals were spread everywhere in the time of Charlemagne. In these, Romans, the better to rob you of your liberty, the bishops are deprived of theirs; it is decreed that the bishop of Rome shall be their only judge. Certainly, if he is the sovereign of the bishops, he should soon be yours; and that is what happened. These false Decretals abolished the Councils, and even abolished your Senate, which became merely a court of justice, subject to the will of a priest. Here is the real source of the humiliation you have suffered. Your rights and privileges, so long maintained by your wisdom, could be wrested from you only by untruth. Only by lying to God and men did they succeed in making slaves of you; but they have never extinguished the love of liberty in your hearts. The greater the tyranny, the greater is that love. The sacred name of liberty is still heard in your conversations and gatherings, and in the very antechamber of the pope.

ARTICLE IX

Cæsar was but your dictator; Augustus was content to be your general, consul, and tribune; Tiberius, Caligula, and Nero left you your elections, your prerogatives, and your dignities; even the barbarians respected them. You maintained your municipal government. Not by the authority of your bishop, Gregory III., but of your own decision, you offered the dignity of patrician to the great Charles Martel, master of his king, conqueror of the Saracens in the year 741 of our faulty vulgar era.

Believe not that it was the Bishop Leo III. who made Charlemagne emperor; it is an absurd romance of the secretary Eginhard, a vile flatterer of the popes, who had won him. By what right and in what way could a subject bishop make an emperor? Emperors were created only by the people, or by the armies that took the place of the people.

It was you, people of Rome, who used your rights; you who would no longer depend on a Greek emperor, who gave you no aid; you who appointed Charlemagne, or he would have been a usurper. The annalists of the time agree that all was arranged by Carolo and your leading officers, as is, indeed, most probable. Your bishop's only share in it was to conduct an empty ceremony and receive rich presents. The only authority he had in your city was that of the prestige attaching to his mitre, his clergy, and his ability.

But while you gave yourselves to Charlemagne, you retained the election of your officers. The police was in your hands; you kept possession of the mole of Adrian, so absurdly called in later times the Castello Sant' Angelo; and you were not wholly enslaved until your bishops seized that fortress.

They made their way step by step to that supreme greatness, so expressly forbidden them by him whom they call their god, and of whom they dare to call themselves the vicars. They had never any jurisdiction in Rome under the Othos. Excommunication and intrigue were their sole arms; and even when, in an age of anarchy, they became the real sovereigns, they never dared to assume the title. I defy the astutest of those fabricators of titles who abound in your court to find a single one in which the pope is described as prince by the grace of God. A strange princedom, when one fears to avow it !

The imperial cities of Germany, which have bishops, are free; and you, Romans, are not. The archbishop of Cologne has not even the right to sleep in that city; and your pope will hardly allow you to sleep in your own. The sultan of the Turks is far less despotic at Constantinople than the pope has become at Rome.

You perish miserably in the shade of superb colonnades. Your noble and faded paintings, and your dozen gems of ancient sculpture, bring you neither a good dinner nor a good bed. The opulence is for your masters : the indigence is for you. The lot of a slave among the ancient Romans was a hundred times better than yours. *He* might acquire a large fortune; *you* are born serfs, you die serfs, and the only oil you have is that of the Last Anointing. Slaves in body and in soul, your tyrants do not even allow you to read, in your own tongue, the book on which they say your religion is founded.

Awake, Romans, at the call of liberty, truth, and nature. The cry rings over Europe. You must hear it. Break the chains that bind your generous hands— the chains forged by tyranny in the den of imposture.

THE SERMON OF THE FIFTY

FIFTY cultivated, pious, and reasonable persons have, for a year past, met every Sunday in a large commercial town. They have prayers, and then a member of the society gives a discourse. They afterwards dine, and a collection for the poor is made after dinner. Each presides in turn, and it is the duty of the president to offer the prayer and give the sermon. Here are one of the prayers and one of the sermons.

If the seed of these words fall on good soil, it will assuredly bear fruit.

PRAYER

God of all the globes and stars, the one prayer that it is meet to offer to you is submission. How can we ask anything of him who arranged and enchained all things from the beginning? Yet if it is permitted to expose our needs to a father, preserve in our hearts this feeling of submission and a pure religion. Keep from us all superstition. Since there are those who insult you with unworthy sacrifices, abolish those infamous mysteries. Since there are those who dishonour the divinity with absurd fables, may those fables perish for ever. If the days of the prince and the magistrate were not numbered from all eternity, give them length of days. Preserve the purity of our ways, the friendship of our brethren for each other, their goodwill towards all men, their obedience to the laws, and their wisdom in private life. Let them live and die in the worship of one God, the rewarder of good, the punisher of evil; a

God that could not be born or die, nor have associates, but who has too many rebellious children in this world.

SERMON

My brethren, religion is the secret voice of God speaking to men. It ought to unite men, not divide them; hence every religion that belongs to one people only is false. Ours is, in principle, that of the whole universe; for we worship a supreme being as all nations do, we practise the justice which all nations teach, and we reject all the untruths with which the nations reproach each other. At one with them in the principle which unites them, we differ from them in the things about which they are in conflict.

The point on which all men of all times agree must be the centre of truth, and the points on which they all differ must be standards of falsehood. Religion must conform to morality, and, like it, be universal; hence every religion whose dogmas offend against morality is certainly false. It is under this twofold aspect of perversity and falseness that we will, in this discourse, examine the books of the Hebrews and of those who have succeeded them. Let us first see if these books conform to morality; we shall then see if they have any shade of probability. The first two points will deal with the Old Testament; the third will discuss the New.

First Point

You know, my brethren, what horror fell on us when we read together the writings of the Hebrews, confining our attention to those features which offend against purity, charity, good faith, justice, and reason—features which one not only finds in every chapter, but, unhappily, one finds consecrated in them.

First, to say nothing of the extravagant injustice

which they venture to ascribe to the supreme being, in endowing a serpent with speech in order to seduce a woman and her innocent posterity, let us run over in succession all the historical horrors which outrage nature and good sense. One of the patriarchs, Lot, the nephew of Abraham, receives in his house two angels disguised as pilgrims; the inhabitants of Sodom entertain impure desires of these angels; Lot, who had two daughters promised in marriage, offers to abandon them to the people instead of the two strangers. These young women must have been strangely familiar with evil ways, since the first thing they do after the destruction of their town by a rain of fire, and after their mother has been changed into a pillar of salt, is to intoxicate their father on two consecutive nights, in order to sleep with him in succession. It is an imitation of the ancient Arabic legend of Cyniras and Myrrha. But in this more decent legend Myrrha is punished for her crime, while the daughters of Lot are rewarded with what is, in Jewish eyes, the greatest and dearest blessing: they become the mothers of a numerous posterity.

We will not insist on the falsehood of Isaac, the father of the just, who says that his wife is his sister; whether he was merely repeating the falsehood of Abraham, or Abraham was really guilty of taking his sister to wife. But let us dwell for a moment on the patriarch Jacob, who is offered to us as a model man. He compels his brother, who is dying of hunger, to give up his birthright for a dish of lentils. He afterwards deceives his aged father on his death-bed. After deceiving his father, he deceives and robs his father-in-law Laban. Not content with wedding two sisters, he lies with all his servants; and God blesses this licentiousness and trickery. Who are the children of such a father? His daughter Dinah pleases a prince of Sichem, and it is probable that she loves the prince, since she lies with him. The prince asks her in marriage, and she is promised on condition that he and all his people are circumcised. The prince accepts the condition; but as soon as he and his people undergo this painful operation—which, nevertheless, leaves them strong enough to defend themselves—Jacob's family murder all the men of Sichem and enslave their women and children.

We have in our infancy heard the story of Pelopæus. This incestuous abomination is repeated in Judah, the patriarch and father of the first tribe. He lies with his daughter-in-law, and then wishes to have her killed. The book declares that then Joseph, a child of this vagabond family, is sold into Egypt, and that, foreigner as he is, he is made first minister as a reward for explaining a dream. What a first minister he was, compelling a whole nation to enslave itself, during a time of famine, to obtain food! What magistrate among us would, in time of famine, dare to propose so abominable a bargain, and what nation would accept it? Let us not stay to examine how seventy members of the family of Joseph, who settled in Egypt, could in two hundred and fifteen years increase to six hundred thousand fighting men, without counting the women, old men, and children, which would make a total of more than two millions. Let us not discuss how it is that the text has four hundred and thirty years, when the same text has given two hundred and fifteen. The infinite number of contradictions, which are the seal of imposture, is not the point which we are considering. Let us likewise pass over the ridiculous prodigies of Moses and of Pharaoh's magicians, and all the miracles wrought to give the Jewish people a wretched bit of poor country, which they afterwards purchase by blood and crime, instead of giving them the fertile soil of Egypt, where they were. Let us confine ourselves to the frightful iniquity of their ways.

Their God had made a thief of Jacob, and he now makes thieves of the entire people. He orders his people to steal and take away with them all the gold and silver vessels and utensils of the Egyptians. Behold these wretches, to the number of six hundred thousand fighting men, instead of taking up arms like men of spirit, flying like brigands led by their God. If their God had wished to give them a good country, he might have given them Egypt. He does not, however; he leads them into a desert. They might have fled by the shortest route, yet they go far out of their way to cross the Red Sea dry-foot. After this fine miracle Moses' own brother makes them another god, and this god is a calf. To punish his brother Moses commands certain priests to kill their sons, brothers, and fathers; and they kill twenty-three thousand Jews, who let themselves be slain like cattle.

After this butchery it is not surprising to hear that this abominable people sacrifices human victims to its god, whom it calls Adonai, borrowing the name of Adonis from the Phœnicians. The twenty-ninth verse of chapter xxvii. of Leviticus expressly forbids the redemption of those who are destined for sacrifice, and it is in virtue of this cannibalistic law that Jephthah, some time afterwards, offers up his own daughter.

It was not enough to slay twenty-three thousand men for a calf; we have again twenty-four thousand sacrificed for having intercourse with idolatrous women. It is, my brethren, a worthy prelude and example of persecution on the ground of religion.

This people advances in the deserts and rocks of Palestine. Here is your splendid country, God says to them. Slay all the inhabitants, kill all the male infants, make an end of their married women, keep the young girls for yourselves. All this is carried out to the letter, according to the Hebrew books; and we should shudder at the account, if the text did not add that the Jews found in the camp of the Midianites 675,000 sheep, 62,000 cattle, 61,000 asses, and 32,000

girls.   Happily, the absurdity undoes the barbarism.
Once more, however, I am not concerned here with
what is ridiculous and impossible; I select only what
is execrable.   Having passed the Jordan dry-shod,
as they crossed the sea, we find our people in the
promised land.

The first person to let in this holy people, by an act
of treachery, is Rahab, a strange character for God
to associate with himself.   He levels the walls of
Jericho at the sound of the trumpet; the holy people
enters the town—to which it had no right, on its own
confession—and slays the men, women, and children.
Let us pass over the other carnages, the crucifixion
of kings, the supposed wars against the giants of
Gaza and Ascalon, and the murder of those who
could not pronounce the word " Shibboleth."

Listen to this fine story.

A Levite, with his wife, arrives on his ass at Gibeah,
in the tribe of Benjamin.   Some of the Benjamites,
who are bent on committing the sin of sodomy with
the Levite, turn their brutality upon the woman, who
dies of the violence.   Were the culprits punished?
Not at all.   The eleven tribes slaughtered the whole
tribe of Benjamin; only six hundred men escaped.
But the eleven tribes are afterwards sorry to see a
tribe perish, and, to restore it, they exterminate
the inhabitants of one of their own towns in order
to take from it six hundred girls, whom they give to
the six hundred Benjamites who survive to perpetuate
this splendid race.

How many crimes committed in the name of the
Lord !   We will give only that of the man of God
(Ehud).   The Jews, having come so far to conquer,
are subject to the Philistines.   In spite of the Lord,
they have sworn obedience to King Eglon.   A holy
Jew, named Ehud, asks permission to speak in private
with the king on the part of God.   The king does not
fail to grant the audience.   Ehud assassinates him,
and his example has been used many times by

Christians to betray, destroy, or massacre so many
sovereigns.

At length this chosen nation, which had thus been
directed by God himself, desires to have a king;
which greatly displeases the priest Samuel. The
first Jewish king renews the custom of immolating
men. Saul prudently enjoined that his soldiers
should not eat on the day they fought the Philistines,
to give them more vigour; he swore to the Lord that
he would immolate to him any man who ate. Happily,
the people were wiser than he; they would not suffer
the king's son to be sacrificed for eating a little honey.
But listen, my brethren, to this most detestable, yet
most consecrated, act. It is said that Saul takes
prisoner a king of the country, named Agag. He did
not kill his prisoner; he acted as is usual in humane
and civilised nations. What happened? The Lord
is angry, and Samuel, priest of the Lord, says to
Saul: "You are reprobate for having spared a king
who surrendered to you." And the priestly butcher
at once cuts Agag into pieces. What would you
say, my brethren, if, when the Emperor Charles V.
had a French king in his hands, his chaplain came and
said to him: "You are damned for not killing
Francis I.," and proceeded to cut the French king to
pieces before the eyes of the Emperor?

What will you say of the holy King David, the king
who found favour in the eyes of the God of the Jews,
and merited to be an ancestor of the Messiah? This
good king is at first a brigand, capturing and pillaging
all he finds. Among others, he despoils a rich man
named Nabal, marries his wife, and flies to King
Achish. During the night he descends upon the
villages of King Achish, his benefactor, with fire and
sword. He slaughters men, women, and children,
says the sacred text, lest there be anyone left to take
the news. When he is made king he ravishes the
wife of Uriah, and has the husband put to death;
and it is from this adulterous homicide that the

Messiah—God himself—descends.   What blasphemy!
This David, who thus becomes an ancestor of God as
a reward of his horrible crime, is punished for the one
good and wise action which he did.   There is no
good and prudent prince who ought not to know the
number of his people, as the shepherd should know the
number of his flock.   David has them enumerated—
though we are not told what the number was—and
for making this wise and useful enumeration a
prophet comes from God to give him the choice of
war, pestilence, or famine.

Let us not linger, my dear brethren, over the
numberless barbarities of the kings of Judah and
Israel—their murders and outrages, mixed up always
with ridiculous stories; though even the ridiculous
in them is always bloody, and not even the prophet
Elisha is free from barbarism.   This worthy devotee
has forty children devoured by bears because the
innocent youngsters had called him "bald."   Let
us leave this atrocious nation in the Babylonian
captivity and in its bondage to the Romans, with
all the fine promises of their god Adonis or Adonai,
who had so often promised the Jews the sovereignty
of the earth.   In fine, under the wise government
of the Romans, a king is born to the Hebrews.   You
know, my brethren, who this king, *shilo*, or Messiah
is; it is he who, after being at first numbered among
the prophets without a mission, who, though not
priests, made a profession of inspiration, was, after
some centuries, regarded as a god.   We need go no
farther; let us see on what pretexts, what facts,
what miracles, what prophecies—in a word, on what
foundation, this disgusting and abominable history
is based.

Second Point

O God, if thou thyself didst descend upon the earth,
and didst command me to believe this tissue of murders,
thefts, assassinations, and incests committed by thy

order and in thy name, I should say to thee : No ;
thy sanctity cannot ask me to acquiesce in these
horrible things that outrage thee. Thou seekest,
no doubt, to try me.

How, then, my virtuous and enlightened hearers,
could we accept this frightful story on the wretched
evidence which is offered in support of it ?

Run briefly over the books that have been falsely
attributed to Moses. I say falsely, since it is not
possible for Moses to have written about things that
happened long after his time. None of us would
believe that the memoirs of William, Prince of Orange,
were written with his own hand if there were allusions
in these memoirs to things that happened after
his death. Let us see what is narrated in the name of
Moses. First, God created the light, which he calls
" day " ; then the darkness, which he calls " night,"
and it was the first day. Thus there were days before
the sun was made.

On the sixth day God makes man and woman ;
but the author, forgetting that woman has been made
already, afterwards derives her from one of Adam's
ribs. Adam and Eve are put in a garden from
which four rivers issue ; and of these rivers there
are two, the Euphrates and the Nile, which have
their sources a thousand miles from each other. The
serpent then spoke like a man ; it was the most
cunning of animals. It persuades the woman to eat
an apple, and so has her driven from paradise. The
human race increases, and the children of God fall
in love with the daughters of men. There were giants
on the earth, and God was sorry that he had made
man. He determined to exterminate him by a flood ;
but wished to save Noah, and ordered him to make a
vessel of poplar wood, three hundred cubits in
length. Into this vessel were to be brought seven
pairs of all the clean animals, and two pairs of the
unclean. It was necessary to feed them during the
ten months that the water covered the earth. You

can imagine what would be needed to feed fourteen elephants, fourteen camels, fourteen buffaloes, and as many horses, asses, deer, serpents, ostriches—in a word, more than two thousand species.[1] You will ask me whence came the water to cover the whole earth and rise fifteen cubits above the highest mountains? The text replies that it came from the cataracts of heaven. Heaven knows where these cataracts are. After the deluge God enters into an alliance with Noah and with all the animals; and in confirmation of this alliance he institutes the rainbow.

Those who wrote these things were not, as you perceive, great physicists. However, here is Noah with a religion given to him by God, and this religion is neither Jewish nor Christian. The posterity of Noah seeks to build a tower that shall reach to heaven. A fine enterprise! But God fears it, and causes the workers suddenly to speak several different tongues, and they disperse. The whole **is** written in this ancient oriental vein.

A rain of fire converts towns into a lake; Lot's wife is changed into a salt-statue; Jacob fights all night with an angel, and is hurt in the leg; Joseph, sold as a slave into Egypt, is made first minister because he explains a dream. Seventy members of the family settle in Egypt, and in two hundred and fifteen years, as we saw, multiply into two millions. It is these two million Hebrews who fly from Egypt and go the longest way in order to have the pleasure of crossing the sea dry-shod.

But there is nothing surprising about this miracle. Pharaoh's magicians performed some very fine miracles. Like Moses, they changed a rod into a serpent, which is a very simple matter. When Moses changed water into blood, they did the same. When he brought frogs into existence, they imitated him. But they were beaten when it came to the plague

---

[1] More than a million species, on modern estimates.—J. M.

of lice; on that subject the Jews knew more than other nations.

In the end Adonai causes the death of each first-born in Egypt in order to allow his people to leave in peace. The sea divides to let them pass; it was the least that could be done on such an occasion. The remainder is on the same level. The people cry out in the desert. Some of the husbands complain of their wives; at once a water is found which causes any woman who has forfeited her honour to swell and burst. They have neither bread nor paste; quails and manna are rained on them. Their garments last forty years, and grow with the children. Apparently clothes descend from heaven for the new-born children.

A prophet of the district seeks to curse the people, but his ass opposes the project, together with an angel, and the ass speaks very reasonably and at great length to the prophet.

When they attack a town, the walls fall at the sound of trumpets; just as Amphion built walls to the sound of the flute. But the finest miracle is when five Amorite kings—that is to say, five village sheiks—attempt to oppose the ravages of Joshua. They are not merely vanquished and cut to pieces, but the Lord sends a great rain of stones upon the fugitives. Even that is not enough. A few escape, and, in order to give the Israelites time to pursue them, nature suspends its eternal laws. The sun halts at Gibeon, and the moon at Aijalon. We do not quite understand how the moon comes in, but the books of Joshua leave no room for doubt as to the fact. Now let us pass to other miracles, and go on to Samson, who is depicted as a famous plunderer, a friend of God. Samson routs a thousand Philistines with the jawbone of an ass, because he is not shaved, and ties by the tails three hundred foxes which he found in a certain place.

There is hardly a page that does not contain similar stories. In one place it is the shade of Samuel

appearing in response to the voice of a witch; in
another it is the shadow on a sun-dial (assuming that
these miserable folk had sun-dials) receding ten degrees
at the prayer of Hezekiah, who prudently asks for this
sign.   God gives him the alternatives of advancing or
retarding the hour, and Dr. Hezekiah thinks that it is
not difficult to put the shadow on, but very difficult
to put it back.

Elias rises to heaven in a fiery chariot; children
sing in a fiery furnace.   I should never come to an
end if I wished to enter into all the details of the
unheard-of extravagances that swarm in this book.
Never was common sense assailed with such indecency
and fury.

Such is, from one end to the other, the Old Testament, the father of the New, a father who disavows
his child, and regards it as a rebellious bastard; for
the Jews, faithful to the law of Moses, regard with
detestation the Christianity that has been reared on
the ruins of their law.   The Christians, however,
have with great subtlety sought to justify the New
Testament by the Old.   The two religions thus fight
each other with the same weapons; they invoke
the same prophets and appeal to the same predictions.

Will the ages to come, which will have seen the
passing of these follies, yet may, unhappily, witness
the rise of others not less unworthy of God and men,
believe that Judaism and Christianity based their
claims on such foundations and such prophecies?
What prophecies! Listen. The prophet Isaiah is
summoned by Ahaz, king of Judah, to make certain
predictions to him, in the vain and superstitious
manner of the East.   These prophets were, as you
know, men who earned more or less of a living by
divination; there were many like them in Europe
in the last century, especially among the common
people. King Ahaz, besieged in Jerusalem by
Shalmaneser, who had taken Samaria, demanded of

the soothsayer a prophecy and a sign. Isaiah said to him : This is the sign :—

" A girl will conceive, and will bear a child who shall be called Emmanuel. He shall eat butter and honey until the day when he shall reject evil and choose good; and before this child is of age, the land which thou detestest shall be forsaken by its two kings; and the Lord shall hiss for the flies that are on the banks of the streams of Egypt and Assyria; and the Lord will take a razor, and shave the King of Assyria; he will shave his head and the hair of his feet."

After this splendid prophecy, recorded in Isaiah, but of which there is not a word in Kings, the prophet orders him first to write on a large roll, which they hasten to seal. He urges the king to press to the plunder of his enemies, and then ensures the birth of the predicted child. Instead of calling it Emmanuel, however, he gives it the name of Maher Salabas. This, my brethren, is the passage which Christians have distorted in favour of their Christ; this is the prophecy that set up Christianity. The girl to whom the prophet ascribes a child is incontestably the Virgin Mary.[1] Maher Salabas is Jesus Christ. As to the butter and honey, I am unaware what it means. Each soothsayer promises the Jews deliverance when they are captive; and this deliverance is, according to the Christians, the heavenly Jerusalem, and the Church of our time. Prophecy is everything with the Jews; with the Christians miracle is everything, and all the prophecies are figures of Jesus Christ.

Here, my brethren, is one of these fine and striking prophecies. The great prophet Ezekiel sees a wind from the north, and four animals, and wheels of chrysolite full of eyes; and the Lord says to him : " Rise, eat a book, and then depart."

---

[1] As is well known, the word " virgin " is a wilful mis-translation of the text of Isaiah. " Girl " is the correct translation.—J. M.

The Lord orders him to sleep three hundred and ninety days on the left side, and then forty on the right side. The Lord binds him with cords; he was certainly a man that needed binding. What follows in Ezekiel is very distasteful.

But we need not waste our time in assailing all the disgusting and abominable dreams which are the subject of controversy between the Jews and Christians. We will be content to deplore the most pitiful blindness that has ever darkened the mind of man. Let us hope that this blindness will pass like so many others, and let us proceed to the New Testament, a worthy sequel to what has gone before.

Third Point

Vain was it that the Jews were a little more enlightened in the time of Augustus than in the barbaric ages of which we have spoken. Vainly did the Jews begin to recognise the immortality of the soul, a dogma unknown to Moses, and the idea of God rewarding the just after death and punishing the wicked, a dogma equally unknown to Moses. Reason none the less penetrated this miserable people, from whom issued the Christian religion, which has proved the source of so many divisions, civil wars, and crimes; which has caused so much blood to flow; and which is broken into so many sects in the corner of the earth where it rules.

There were at all times among the Jews people of the lowest order, who made prophecies in order to distinguish themselves from the populace. We deal here with the one who has become best known, and has been turned into a god; we give a brief account of his career, as it is described in the books called the Gospels. We need not seek to determine when these books were written; it is evident that they were written after the fall of Jerusalem. You know how absurdly the four authors contradict each other. It is a demonstrative proof that they are wrong.

We do not, however, need many proofs to demolish this miserable structure. We will be content with a short and faithful account.

In the first place, Jesus is described as a descendant of Abraham and David, and the writer Matthew counts forty-two generations in two thousand years. In his list, however, we find only forty-one, and in the genealogical tree which he borrows from *Kings* he blunders clumsily in making Josiah the father of Jechoniah.

Luke also gives a genealogy, but he assigns forty-nine generations after Abraham, and they are entirely different generations. To complete the absurdity, these generations belong to Joseph, and the evangelists assure us that Jesus was not the son of Joseph. Would one be received in a German chapter on such proofs of nobility? Yet there is question here of the son of God, and God himself is the author of the book!

Matthew says that when Jesus, King of the Jews, was born in a stable in the town of Bethlehem, three magi or kings saw his star in the East, and followed it, until it halted over Bethlehem; and that King Herod, hearing these things, caused all the children under two years of age to be put to death. Could any horror be more ridiculous? Matthew adds that the father and mother took the child into Egypt, and remained there until the death of Herod. Luke says precisely the contrary; he observes that Joseph and Mary remained peacefully at Bethlehem for six weeks, then went to Jerusalem, and from there to Nazareth; and that they went every year to Jerusalem.

The evangelists contradict each other in regard to the time of the life of Jesus, his miracles, the night of the supper, and the day of his death—in a word, in regard to nearly all the facts. There were forty-nine gospels composed by the Christians of the first few centuries, and these were still more flagrant in their contradictions. In the end, the four which we have were selected. Even if they were in harmony, what folly, what misery, what puerile and odious things they contain !

The first adventure of Jesus, son of God, is to be taken up by the devil; the devil, who makes no appearance in the books of Moses, plays a great part in the Gospels. The devil, then, takes God up a mountain in the desert. From there he shows him all the kingdoms of the earth. Where is this mountain from which one can see so many lands? We do not know.

John records that Jesus goes to a marriage-feast, and changes water into wine; and that he drives from the precincts of the temple those who were selling the animals of the sacrifices ordered in the Jewish law.

All diseases were at that time regarded as possession by the devil, and Jesus makes it the mission of his apostles to expel devils. As he goes along, he delivers one who was possessed by a legion of devils, and he makes these devils enter a herd of swine, which cast themselves into the sea of Tiberias. We may suppose that the owners of the swine, who were not Jews apparently, were not pleased with this comedy. He heals a blind man, and the blind man sees men as if they were trees. He wishes to eat figs in winter, and, not finding any on a tree, he curses the tree and causes it to wither; the text prudently adds : " For it was not the season of figs."

He is transformed during the night, and causes Moses and Elias to appear. Do the stories of romancers even approach these absurdities? At length, after constantly insulting the Pharisees, calling them " races of vipers," " whitened sepulchres," etc., he is handed over by them to justice, and executed with two thieves; and the historians are bold enough to tell us that at his death the earth was darkened at midday, and at a time of full moon. As if every writer of the time would not have mentioned so strange a miracle.

After that it is a small matter to make him rise from the dead and predict the end of the world; which, however, has not happened.

The sect of Jesus lingers in concealment; fanaticism increases. At first they dare not make a God of this man, but they soon take courage. Some Platonic metaphysic amalgamates with the Nazaræan sect, and Jesus becomes the logos, the word of God, then consubstantial with God his father. The Trinity is invented; and, in order to have it accepted, the first gospels are falsified.

A passage is added in regard to this truth, and the historian Josephus is falsified and made to speak of Jesus, though Josephus is too serious an historian to mention such a man. They go so far as to forge sybilline books. In a word, there is no kind of trickery, fraud, and imposture that the Nazaræans do not adopt. At the end of three years they succeeded in having Jesus recognised as a god. Not content with this extravagance, they go so far as to locate their god in a bit of paste. While their god is eaten by mice and digested, they hold that there is no such thing as bread in the host; that God has, at the word of a man, put himself in the place of the bread. All kinds of superstitions flood the Church; plunder is predominant in it; indulgences, benefices, and all kinds of spiritual things, are put up for sale.

The sect splits into a multitude of sects; age after age they fight and slaughter each other. At every dispute kings and princes are massacred.

Such, my dear brethren, is the fruit of the tree of the Cross, the power that has been declared divine.

For this they have dared to bring God upon the earth; to commit Europe for ages to murder and brigandage. It is true that our fathers have in part shaken off this frightful yoke, and rid themselves of some errors and superstitions. But how imperfect they have left the work! Everything tells us that it is time to complete it; to destroy utterly the idol of which we have as yet broken only a finger or two. Numbers of theologians have already embraced Socinianism (Unitarianism), which comes near to the worship of one God, freed from superstition. England, Germany, and the provinces of France are full of wise doctors, who ask only the opportunity to break away. There are great numbers in other countries. Why persist in teaching what we do not believe, and make ourselves guilty before God of this great sin?

We are told that the people need mysteries, and must be deceived. My brethren, dare any one commit this outrage on humanity? Have not our fathers already taken from the people their transubstantiation, auricular confession, indulgences, exorcisms, false miracles, and ridiculous statues? Are not the people accustomed to the deprivation of this food of superstition? We must have the courage to go a few steps farther. The people are not so weak of mind as is thought; they will easily admit a wise and simple cult of one God, such as was professed, it is said, by Abraham and Noah, and by all the sages of antiquity, and as is found among the educated people of China. We seek not to despoil the clergy of what the liberality of their followers has given them; we wish them, since most of them secretly laugh at the untruths they teach, to join us in preaching the truth. Let them observe that, while they now offend and dishonour the deity, they would, if they follow us, glorify him. What incalculable good would be done by that happy change? Princes and magistrates would be better obeyed, the people would be tranquil, the spirit of division and hatred would be expelled. They would offer to God, in peace, the first fruits of their work. There would assuredly be more righteousness on the earth, for many weak-minded folk who hear contempt expressed daily for the Christian superstition, and know that it is ridiculed by the priests themselves, thoughtlessly imagine that there is no such thing as religion, and abandon themselves to excesses.   But when they learn that the Christian sect is really only a perversion of natural religion; when reason, freed from its chains, teaches the people that there is but one God; that this God is the common parent of all men, who are brothers; that, as brothers, they must be good and just to each other, and practise every virtue; that God, being good and just, must reward virtue and punish crime; then assuredly, my brethren, men will gain in righteousness as they lose in superstition.

We begin by giving this example in secret, and we trust that it will be followed in public.

May the great God who hears me—a God who certainly could not be born of a girl, nor die on a gibbet, nor be eaten in a morsel of paste, nor have inspired this book with its contradictions, follies, and horrors—may this God, creator of all worlds, have pity on the sect of the Christians who blaspheme him. May he bring them to the holy and natural religion, and shower his blessing on the efforts we make to have him worshipped.   Amen.

HOMILY ON SUPERSTITION

My Brethren,

You are aware that all prominent nations have set up a public cult. Men have at all times assembled to deal with their interests and communicate their needs, and it was quite natural that they should open these meetings with some expression of the respect and love which they owe to the author of their lives. This homage has been compared to the respect which children pay to their father, and subjects to their sovereign. These are but feeble images of the worship of God. The relations of man to man have no proportion to the relation of the creature to the supreme being; there is no affinity between them. It would even be blasphemy to render homage to God in the form of a monarch. A ruler of the whole earth —if there could be such a person, and all men were so unhappy as to be subject to one man—would be but a worm of the earth, commanding other worms of the earth; he would still be infinitely lower than the deity. In republics, moreover, which are unquestionably earlier than any monarchy, how could God be conceived in the shape of a king? If it be necessary to represent God in any sensible form, the idea of a father, defective as it is, would seem to be the best fitted to our weakness.

But emblems of the deity were one of the first sources of superstition. As soon as we made God in our own image, the divine cult was perverted. Having dared to represent God in the form of a man, our wretched imagination, which never halts, ascribed to him all the vices of a man. We regarded him only as a powerful master, and we charged him with abuse of power; we described him as proud, jealous, angry, vindictive, maleficent, capricious, pitilessly destructive, a despoiler of some to enrich others, with no other reason but his will. Our ideas are confined to the things about us; we conceive hardly anything except by similitudes; and so, when the earth was covered with tyrants, God was regarded as the first of tyrants. It was much worse when the deity was presented in emblems taken from animals and plants. God became an ox, serpent, crocodile, ape, cat, or lamb; bellowing, hissing, devouring, and being devoured.

The superstition of almost all nations has been so horrible that, did not the monuments of it survive, it would be impossible to believe the accounts of it. The history of the world is the history of fanaticism.

Have there been innocent superstitions among the monstrous forms that have covered the earth? Can we not distinguish between poisons which have been used as remedies and poisons which have retained their murderous nature? If I mistake not, here is an inquiry worth the close attention of reasonable men.

A man does good to his fellows and brothers. One man destroys carnivorous beasts; another invents arts by the force of his genius. They are, on that account, regarded as higher in the favour of God than other men, as children of God; they become demi-gods, or secondary gods, when they die. They are proposed to other men, not merely as models, but as objects of worship. He who worships Hercules and Perseus is incited to imitate them. Altars are the reward of genius and courage. I see in that only an error which leads to good. In that case they are deceived to their own advantage. How could we reproach the ancient Romans if they had raised to the rank of secondary gods only such men as Scipio, Titus, Trajan, and Marcus Aurelius?

There is an infinite distance between God and man. We agree; but if, in the system of the ancients, the

human soul was regarded as a finite portion of the
infinite intelligence, sinking back into the great whole
without adding to it ; if it be supposed that God dwelt
in the soul of Marcus Aurelius, since his soul was
superior to others in virtue during life ; why may we
not suppose that it is still superior when it is separated
from its mortal body ?

Our brothers of the Roman Catholic Church (for
all men are brothers) have filled heaven with demi-
gods, which they call " saints." Had they always
chosen them wisely, we may candidly allow that their
error would have been of service to human nature.
We pour on them our disdain only because they
honour an Ignatius, the knight of the Virgin, a
Dominic, the persecutor, or a Francis, fanatical to
the pitch of madness, who goes naked, speaks to
animals, catechises a wolf, and makes himself a wife
of snow. We cannot forgive Jerome, the learned but
faulty translator of the Jewish books, for having, in
his history of the fathers of the desert, demanded our
respect for a St. Pacomius, who paid his visits on the
back of a crocodile. We are especially angered when
we see that Rome has canonised Gregory VII., the
incendiary of Europe.

It is otherwise with the cult that is paid in France
to King Louis IX., who was just and courageous. If
it is too much to invoke him, it is not too much to
revere him. It is but to say to other princes :
Imitate his virtues.

I go farther. Suppose there had been placed in
some church the statue of Henry IV., who won his
kingdom with the valour of Alexander and the
clemency of Titus, who was good and compassionate,
chose the best ministers and was his own first minister ;
suppose that, in spite of his weaknesses, he received a
homage beyond the respect which we owe to great
men. What harm would be done ? It would assuredly be better to bend the knee before him than
before this crowd of unknown saints, whose very

names have become a subject of opprobrium and ridicule. I agree that it would be a superstition, but a superstition that could do no harm; a patriotic enthusiasm, not a pernicious fanaticism. If man is born to error, let us wish him virtuous errors.

The superstition that we must drive from the earth is that which, making a tyrant of God, invites men to become tyrants. He who was the first to say that we must detest the wicked put a sword in the hands of all who dared to think themselves faithful. He who was the first to forbid communication with those who were not of his opinion rang the tocsin of civil war throughout the earth.

I believe what seems to reason impossible—in other words, I believe what I do not believe—and therefore I must hate those who boast that they believe an absurdity opposed to mine. Such is the logic—such, rather, is the madness—of the superstitious. To worship, love, and serve the supreme being, and to be of use to men, is nothing; it is indeed, according to some, a false virtue, a " splendid sin," as they call it. Ever since men made it a sacred duty to dispute about what they cannot understand, and made virtue consist in the pronunciation of certain unintelligible words, which everyone attempted to explain, Christian countries have been a theatre of discord and carnage.

You will tell me that this universal pestilence should be imputed to the fury of ambition rather than to that of fanaticism. I answer that it is due to both. The thirst for domination has been assuaged with the blood of fools. I do not aspire to heal men of power of this furious passion to subject the minds of others; it is an incurable disease. Every man would like to see others hastening to serve him; and, that he may be the better served, he will, if he can, make them believe that their duty and their happiness are to be slaves. Find me a man with an income of a hundred thousand pounds a year, and with four or five hundred thousand subjects throughout Europe,

who cost him nothing, besides his soldiers, and tell
him that Christ, of whom he is the vicar and imitator,
lived in poverty and humility.   He will reply that the
times are changed, and to prove it he will condemn
you to perish in the flames.   You will neither correct
this man [the Pope] nor a Cardinal de Lorraine, the
simultaneous possessor of seven bishoprics.   What
can one do, then?   Appeal to the people, and, brutal-
ised as they are, they listen and half open their eyes.
They partly throw off the most humiliating yoke that
has ever been borne.   They rid themselves of some of
their errors, and win back a part of their freedom,
that appanage or essence of man of which they had
been robbed.   We cannot cure the powerful of ambition, but we can cure the people of superstition.   We
can, by speech and pen, make men more enlightened
and better.

It is easy to make them see what they have suffered
during fifteen hundred years.   Few people read, but
all may listen.   Listen, then, my brethren, and hear
the calamities which have fallen on earlier generations.

Hardly had the Christians, breathing freely under
Constantine, dipped their hands in the blood of the
virtuous Valeria,[1] daughter, wife, and mother of the
Cæsars, and in the blood of her young son Candidian,
the hope of the Empire; hardly had they put to death
the son of the Emperor Maximin, in his eighth year,
and his daughter in her seventh year; hardly had
these men, who are described as so patient for two
centuries, betrayed their fury at the beginning of the
fourth century, than controversy gave birth to those
civil discords which, succeeding each other without a
moment of relaxation, still agitate Europe.   What are
the subjects of these bloody quarrels?   Subtilties,
my brethren, of which not a trace is to be found in the
Gospel.   They would know whether the Son was
engendered or made; whether he was engendered in

[1] Daughter of the Emperor Diocletian.   Not executed by
Christians.—J. M.

time or before time; whether he is consubstantial with, or like, the Father; whether the divine " monad," as Athanasius puts it, is threefold in three hypostases; whether the Holy Ghost was engendered, or proceeded; whether he proceeds from the Father only, or the Father and the Son; whether Jesus had one will or two, or two natures, or one or two persons.

In a word, from " consubstantiality " to " transubstantiation "—terms equally difficult to pronounce and to understand—everything has been a matter of dispute, and every dispute has caused torrents of blood to flow.

You know how much was shed by our superstitious Mary, daughter of the tyrant Henry VIII., and worthy spouse of the Spanish tyrant Philip II. The throne of Charles I. became a scaffold; he perished ignominiously, after more than two hundred thousand men had been slaughtered for a liturgy.

You know the civil wars of France. A troop of fanatical theologians, called the Sorbonne, declare Henry III. to have forfeited the throne, and at once a theological apprentice assassinates him. The Sorbonne declares the great Henry IV., our ally, incapable of ruling, and twenty murderers rise in succession; until at last, on the mere announcement that the hero is about to protect his former allies against the Pope's followers, a monk—a schoolmaster—plunges a knife in the heart of the most valiant of kings and best of men in the midst of his capital, under the eyes of his people, and in the arms of his friends. And, by an inconceivable contradiction, his memory is revered for ever, and the troop of the Sorbonne which proscribed and excommunicated him and his faithful subjects, and has no right to excommunicate anybody, still survives, to the shame of France.

It is not the ordinary people, my brethren, not the agricultural workers and the ignorant and peaceful artisans, who have raised these ridiculous and fatal

quarrels, the sources of so many horrors and parricides.   There is, unhappily, not one of them that is
not due to the theologians.   Men fed by your labours
in a comfortable idleness, enriched by your sweat
and your misery, struggled for partisans and slaves;
they inspired you with a destructive fanaticism, that
they might be your masters; they made you superstitious, not that you might fear God the more, but
that you might fear them.

The gospel did not say to James, Peter, or Bartholomew :   " Live in opulence; deck yourselves with
honours; walk amid a retinue of guards."   It did not
say to them : " Disturb the world with your incomprehensible questions."   Jesus, my brethren, touched
none of these questions.   Would you be better theologians than he whom you recognise as your one master ?
What !   He said to you : " All consists in loving God
and your neighbour "; yet you would seek something
else.

Is there anyone among you, is there anyone on the
whole earth, who can think that God will examine
him on points of theology, not judge him by his
deeds?

What is a theological opinion?   It is an idea that
may be true or false; but morality has no interest in
it.   It is clear that you should be virtuous, whether
the Holy Ghost proceeds from the Father by spiration,
or from the Father and the Son.   It is not less clear
that you will never understand any proposition of
this nature.   You will never have the least idea how
Jesus could have two natures and two wills in one
person.   If he had wished you to know it, he would
have told you of it.   I choose these examples among a
hundred others, and I pass in silence over other
controversies in order that I may not re-open wounds
that still bleed.

God has given you understanding; he cannot wish
that you should pervert it.   How could a proposition
of which you can never have an idea be necessary to

you? It is a fact of daily experience that God, who gives everything, has given one man more light and more talent than another. It does not offend our good sense that he has chosen to link one man more closely to himself than others; that he has made him a model of reason or virtue. No one can deny that it is possible for God to shower his finest gifts on one of his works. We may, therefore, believe in Jesus as one who taught and practised virtue; but let us take care that, in wishing to go too far beyond that, we do not overturn the whole structure.

The superstitious man puts poison in the most wholesome food; he is an enemy to himself and others. He believes himself the object of eternal vengeance if he eats meat on a certain day; he believes that a long, grey robe, with a pointed hood and a long beard, is much more agreeable to God than a shaven face and a head that retains its hair; he imagines that his salvation is bound up with certain Latin formulæ which he does not understand. He has educated his daughter in these principles. She buries herself in a dungeon as soon as she reaches a marriageable age; she betrays posterity to please God—more guilty, in regard to the human race, than the Hindoo widow, who casts herself on her husband's pyre after bearing him children.

Monks of the southern parts of Europe, self-condemned to a life that is as abject as it is frightful, do not compare yourselves to the penitents of the banks of the Ganges; your austerities do not approach their voluntary sufferings. And think not that God approves in you what you say he condemns in them.

The superstitious man is his own executioner; and he is the executioner of all who do not agree with him. The most infamous informing he calls " fraternal correction." He accuses the simple innocence that is not on its guard, and, in the candour of its heart, has not set a seal upon its lips. He denounces it to those tyrants of souls who laugh alike at the accused and the accuser.

Lastly, the superstitious man becomes a fanatic, and then his zeal becomes capable of all crimes in the name of the Lord.

We live no longer, it is true, in those abominable days when relatives and friends slaughtered each other, when a hundred battles covered the earth with corpses for the sake of some argument of the school; but a few sparks spring every day from the ashes of these vast conflagrations. Princes no longer march to the field at the voice of priests and monks; but citizens persecute each other still in the heart of the towns, and private life is often poisoned with superstition. What would you say of a family whose members were ever ready to fight each other in order to settle in what way their father must be saluted? My friends, the great thing is to love him; you may salute him as you will. Are you brothers only to be divided? Must that which should unite you be always a thing to separate you?

I know not of a single civil war among the Turks on the ground of religion. I say "civil war"; but history tells of no sedition or trouble among them that was due to controversy. Is it because they have fewer pretexts for disputes? Is it because they are by birth less restless and wiser than we? They ask not to what sect you belong, provided that you pay regularly the slight tax. Latin Christians and Greek Christians, Jacobites, Monothelites, Copts, or Protestants—all are welcome to them; whereas there are not three Christian nations that practise this humanity.

Jesus, my brethren, was not superstitious or intolerant; he said not a single word against the cult of the Romans, who surrounded his country. Let us imitate his indulgence, and deserve to experience it from others.

Let us not be disturbed by the barbaric argument

that is often used. I will give it in its full
strength :—

" You believe that a good man may find favour in
the eyes of the being of beings, the God of justice and
mercy, at any time, in any place, in whatever religion
he has spent his short life. We, on the contrary, say
that a man cannot please God unless he be born
among us, or taught by us. It is proved to us that
we are the only persons in the world who are right.
We know that, although God came upon the earth
and died for all men, he will nevertheless show pity
only to our little gathering, and that even among us
there are very few who will escape eternal torment.
Adopt the safer side, then. Enter our little body,
and strive to be one of the elect among us."

Let us thank our brethren who use this language.
Let us congratulate them on being so sure that all
in the world are damned except a few of themselves;
and let us conclude that our sect is better than
theirs by the very fact that it is more reasonable and
humane. The man who says to me, " Believe as I
do, or God will damn thee," will presently say, " Believe as I do, or I shall assassinate thee." Let us
pray God to soften these atrocious hearts and inspire
all his children with a feeling of brotherhood. We
live in an island in which the episcopal sect dominates
from Dover to the Tweed.[1] From there to the last
of the Orkneys presbyterianism holds the field, and
beside these dominant religions are ten or a dozen
others. Go to Italy, and you will find papal despotism
on the throne. In France it is otherwise; France is
already regarded by Rome as half-heretical. Pass to
Switzerland and Germany. You sleep to-night in a
Calvinistic town, to-morrow night in a Papist town,
and the following night in a Lutheran. You go
on to Russia, and find nothing of all this. It
is a different sect. The court is illumined by an

---

[1] The homily is supposed to have been delivered in London.
—J. M.

empress-philosopher. The august Catherine has put reason on the throne, with magnificence and generosity; but the people of her provinces detest alike the Lutherans, Calvinists, and Papists. They would not eat, nor drink from the same glass, with any of them. I ask you, my brethren, what would happen if, in an assembly of all these sectaries, each thought himself authorised by the divine spirit to secure the triumph of his opinions? See you not the swords drawn, the gibbets raised, the fires lit, from one end of Europe to the other? Who is right in this chaos of disputes? Surely the tolerant and beneficent. Do not say that in preaching tolerance we preach indifference. No, my brethren, he who worships God and serves men is not indifferent. The name is more fitting for the superstitious who thinks that God will be pleased with him for uttering unintelligible formulæ, while he is really very indifferent to the lot of his brother, whom he leaves to perish without aid, or abandons in disgrace, or flatters in prosperity, or persecutes if he is of another sect, unsupported and unprotected. The more the superstitious man concentrates upon absurd beliefs and practices, the more indifferent he becomes to the real needs of humanity. Let us remember one of our charitable compatriots. He founded a hospital for old men in his province. He was asked if it was for Papists, Lutherans, Presbyterians, Quakers, Socinians, Anabaptists, Methodists, or Memnonists? He answered: For men.

O God, keep from us the error of atheism which denies thy existence, and deliver us from the superstition that outrages thy existence and fills ours with horror.

HOMILY ON THE INTERPRETATION OF THE OLD TESTAMENT

My Brethren,

Books rule the world, or, at least, those nations in it which have written language; the others do not count. The Zend Avesta, attributed to the first Zoroaster, was the law of the Persians. The Veda and the Shastabad are the law of the Brahmans. The Egyptians were ruled by the books of Thot, who has been called " the first Mercury." The Koran holds sway to-day over Africa, Egypt, Arabia, India, part of Tartary, the whole of Persia, Scythia, Asia Minor, Syria, Thrace, Thessaly, and the whole of Greece as far as the strait which separates Naples and the Empire.[1] The Pentateuch controls the Jews; and, by a singular dispensation of Providence, it rules us to-day. It is, therefore, our duty to read this work together, since it is the foundation of our faith.

When we read the early chapters of the Pentateuch, we must remember that, in speaking thus to the Jews, God deigned to accommodate himself to their intelligence, which was still very crude. It is well known to-day that our earth is but a point in comparison with the space which we, improperly, call the heavens, in which shine a prodigious number of stars, with planets far superior to ours. We know that light was not made before the day, and that it comes to us from the sun. We know that the supposed solid expanse between the upper and the lower waters, which is called the " firmament," [2] is an error

[1] Greece threw off the Turkish yoke in 1827.—J. M.
[2] In the Greek, Latin, and modern Bibles it is " firmament." In the Hebrew text it is " expanse," though other passages show that it refers to the solid vault or firmament of the Babylonians.—J. M.

125

of ancient physics, adopted by the Greeks. But as God was speaking to the Jews, he deigned to stoop low enough to adopt their language. Certainly no one would have understood him in the desert of Horeb if he had said : " I have put the sun in the centre of your world; the little globe of the earth revolves, with other planets, round this great star, which illumines the planets; and the moon turns round the earth in the course of a month. Those other stars which you see are so many suns, presiding over other worlds."

If the eternal geometrician had spoken thus, he would indeed have spoken worthily, as a master who knows his own work; but no Jew would have understood a word of such sublime truths. The Jewish people were stiff of neck and hard of understanding. It was necessary to give coarse food to a coarse people, which could find sustenance only in such food. It seems that this first chapter of *Genesis* was an allegory presented to them by the Holy Spirit, to be interpreted some day by those whom God would deign to fill with his light. That, at least, was the idea of the leading Jews, since it was forbidden to read this book before reaching one's twenty-fifth year, in order that the mind of young folk might be prepared by masters to read it with more intelligence and respect.

These doctors taught that, in the literal sense, the Nile, Euphrates, Tigris, and Araxes did not really rise in the terrestrial paradise; but that the four rivers, which watered it, evidently meant four virtues necessary to man. It was, according to them, clear that the formation of woman from the rib of man was a most striking allegory of the unvarying harmony that ought to be found in marriage; that the souls of married people ought to be united like their bodies. It is a symbol of the peace and fidelity that ought to rule in conjugal society.

The serpent that seduced Eve, and was the most cunning of all animals on the earth, is, if we are to

believe Philo and other writers, a figurative expression of our corrupt desires. The use of speech, which
Scripture assigns to it, is the voice of our passions
speaking to our hearts. God used the allegory of
the serpent because it was very common in the East.
The serpent was considered subtle because it quickly
escapes those who pursue it, and skilfully falls on
those who attack it. Its change of skin was the
symbol of immortality. The Egyptians carried a
silver serpent in their processions. The Phœnicians,
who were neighbours of the Hebrews, had long had
an allegorical fable of a serpent that had made war
on God and man. In fine, the serpent which tempted
Eve has been recognised as the devil, who is ever
seeking to tempt and undo us.

It is true that the idea of a devil falling from
heaven and becoming the enemy of the human race
was known to the Jews only in the course of time;
but the divine author, who knew that this idea would
spread some day, deigned to plant the seed of it in
the early chapters of *Genesis*.

We really know nothing of the fall of the wicked
angels except from these few words in the Epistle of
St. Jude : " Wandering stars, to whom is reserved
the blackness of darkness for ever, of whom Enoch
also, the seventh from Adam, prophesied." It has
been thought that these wandering stars were the
angels transformed into malevolent demons, and we
supply the place of the prophecies of Enoch, the
seventh man after Adam, which we no longer have.
But no matter into what labyrinth learned men may
wander, in trying to explain these incomprehensible
things, we must always understand in an edifying
sense whatever we cannot understand literally.

The ancient Brahmans, as we said, had this theology
many centuries before the Jewish nation came into
existence. The ancient Persians had given names to
the devils long before the Jews did so. You are
aware that in the Pentateuch we do not find the

name of any angel, good or bad. There is no mention of Gabriel, or Raphael, or Satan, or Asmodeus in the Jewish books until long afterwards, when the little people had learned their names during the Babylonian captivity [or the Persian domination]. That shows, at least, that the doctrine of celestial and infernal beings was common to all great nations. You will find it in the book of Job, a precious monument of antiquity. Job is an Arabic character; if the allegory was written in Arabic. There are still, in the Hebrew translation, purely Arabic phrases.[1] Here, then, we have the Hindoos, Persians, Arabs, and Jews successively adopting much the same theology. It is therefore entitled to close attention.

But what is even more clearly entitled to our attention is the morality that ought to result from all this ancient theology. Men, who are not born to be murderers, since God has not armed them like lions and tigers; who are not born to be imposed upon, since they all necessarily love truth; who are not born to be marauding brigands, since God has given equally to them all the fruits of the earth and the wool of the sheep; but who have, nevertheless, become marauders, perjurers, and murderers, are really angels transformed into demons.

Let us, my brethren, always seek in Holy Writ what morality, not what physics, teaches.

Let the ingenious Father Calmet employ his profound sagacity and penetrating logic in discovering the place of the earthly paradise; we may be content to deserve, if we can, the heavenly paradise by the practice of justice, toleration, and kindliness.

"But of the tree of the knowledge of good and evil, thou shalt not eat of it; for in the day that thou eatest thereof thou shalt surely die " (*Gen.* ii. 17).

Interpreters admit that we do not know of any tree that gives knowledge. Adam did not die on the

---

[1] The Rev. Professor Sayce regards *Job* as a piece of north Arabian or Edomite literature, borrowed by the Jews.—J. M.

day on which he ate of it; he lived for nine hundred and thirty years afterwards, the Scripture says. But, alas, what are nine hundred years between two eternities! They are not to be compared with a moment of time, and our days pass like the shadow. Does not this allegory, however, clearly teach us that knowledge, wrongly understood, is able to undo us? The tree of knowledge bears, no doubt, very bitter fruit, since so many learned theologians have been persecutors or persecuted, and many have died a dreadful death. Ah, my brethren, the Holy Spirit wished to show us how dangerous false science is, how it puffs up the heart, and how absurd a learned doctor often is.

It is from this passage that St. Augustine gathered the guilt of all men on account of the disobedience of the first man. He it is who developed the doctrine of original sin. Whether the stain of this sin corrupted our bodies, or steeped the souls which enter them, is an entirely incomprehensible mystery; it warns us at least not to live in crime, if we were born in crime.

" And the Lord set a mark upon Cain, least any finding him should kill him " (*Gen.* iv.).

Here, especially, my brethren, the fathers are opposed to each other. The family of Adam was not yet numerous; Scripture gives him no other children than Abel and Cain, at the time when the former was murdered by his brother. Why is God forced to give Cain a safeguard against any who may find him? Let us be content to observe that God pardons Cain, no doubt after filling him with remorse. Let us profit by the lesson, and not condemn our brethren to frightful torments for small causes. When God is so merciful as to forgive an abominable murder, we may imitate him. The objection is raised that the same God who pardons a cruel murderer damns all men for ever for the transgression of Adam, whose only crime was to eat the forbidden

fruit. To our feeble human reason it seems unjust
for God to punish eternally all the children of the
guilty, not indeed to atone for a murder, but to
expiate what seems an excusable act of disobedience.
This is said to be an intolerable contradiction, which
we cannot admit in an infinitely good being; but it
is only an apparent contradiction. God hands us
over, with our parents and children, to the flames for
the disobedience of Adam; but four thousand years
afterwards he sends Jesus Christ to deliver us, and
he preserves the life of Cain in order to people the
earth: thus he remains in all things the God of
justice and mercy. St. Augustine calls Adam's sin
a " fortunate fault "; but that of Cain was still more
fortunate, since God took care himself to put a
mark of his protection on him.

" A window shalt thou make to the ark, and in a
cubit shalt thou finish it above," etc. (*Gen.* vi. 16).

Here we reach the greatest of all miracles, before
which reason must humble itself and the heart must
break. We know with what bold contempt the in-
credulous rise against the prodigy of a universal
deluge.

It is fruitless for them to object that in the wettest
years we do not get thirty inches of rain; that even
in such a year there are as many regions without rain
as there are flooded regions; that the law of gravity
prevents the ocean from overflowing its bounds;
that if it covered the earth it would leave its bed
dry; that, even if it covered the earth, it could not
rise fifteen cubits above the highest mountains; that
the animals could not reach the ark from America
and southern lands; that seven pairs of clean animals
and two pairs of unclean could not have been put in
twenty arks; that these twenty arks would not have
sufficed to hold the fodder they needed, not merely
for ten months, but for the following year, in which
the earth would be too sodden to produce; that the
carnivorous animals would have died of starvation;

that the eight persons in the ark would not have been able to give the animals their food every day. There is no end to their difficulties. But the whole of them are solved by pointing out that this great event was a miracle—that puts an end to all dispute.

" And they said, Go to, let us build us a city and a tower, whose top may reach unto heaven; and let us make us a name, lest we be scattered abroad upon the face of the whole earth " (*Gen.* xi. 4).

Unbelievers declare that it is possible to make a name, yet be scattered abroad. They ask if men have ever been so stupid as to wish to build a tower as high as the heavens. They say that such a tower would rise into the atmosphere, and that, if you call the atmosphere the heavens, the tower will necessarily be in the heavens if it were no more than twenty feet high; and that, if all men then spoke the same tongue, the wisest thing they could do would be to gather in a common city and prevent a corruption of their tongue. Apparently they were all in their own country, since they were all agreed to build therein. To drive them from their country is tyrannical; to make them suddenly speak new tongues is absurd. Hence, they say, we can only regard the story of the tower of Babel as an oriental romance.

I reply to this blasphemy that, since the miracle is described by an author who has recorded so many other miracles, it ought to be believed, like the others. The works of God cannot be expected to resemble the works of man in any way. The ages of the patriarchs and prophets can have no relation to the ages of ordinary men. God now comes upon the earth no more; but in those days he often came down to carry out his work in person. It is a tradition of all the great nations of antiquity. The Greeks, who had no knowledge of the Jewish books until long after they had been translated into Greek at Alexandria by Hellenising Jews, had believed, before Homer and Hesiod, that the great Zeus and all the other gods came down from the upper air to visit the earth. What lesson may we derive from the general acceptance of this idea? That we are always in the presence of God, and that we must engage in no deed or thought that is not in accord with his justice. In a word, the tower of Babel is no more extraordinary than all the rest. The book is equally authentic in all its parts; we cannot deny one fact without denying all the others. We must bring our proud reason into subjection, whether we regard the story as literally true or as a figure.

"In the same day the Lord made a covenant with Abram, saying: Unto thy seed have I given this land, from the river of Egypt unto the great river, the river Euphrates" (*Gen.* xv. 18).

Unbelievers exclaim triumphantly that the Jews have never owned more than a part of what God promised them. They even think it unjust that the Lord gave them this part. They say that the Jews had not the least right to it; that the former journey of a Chaldæan into a barbaric country could not possibly be a legitimate pretext for invading the country; and that any man who declared himself a descendant of St. Patrick, and came on that account to sack Ireland, saying that he had God's order to do so, would meet with a warm reception. But let us always remember that the times have changed. Let us respect the books of the Jews, and take care not to imitate the Jews. God enjoins no longer what he once commanded.

They ask who this Abraham is, and why the Jewish people is traced to the Chaldæan son of an idolatrous potter, who had no relation to the people of the land of Canaan, and could not understand their language. This Chaldæan, accompanied by a wife who bends under the weight of years, but is still good, reaches Memphis. Why do the couple pass from Memphis to the desert of Gerar? How comes there to be a king in this horrible desert? How is it that the king of Egypt and the king of Gerar both fall in love with the aged [1] spouse of Abraham? These are but historical difficulties; the great thing is to obey God. Holy Scripture always represents Abraham as·unreservedly submissive to the will of the Most High. Let us imitate him, and not dispute so. much.

"And there came two angels to Sodom at even," etc. (*Gen.* xix.).

Here is a stumbling-block for all readers who listen only to their own reason. Two angels—that is to say, two spiritual creatures, two heavenly ministers of God—have earthly bodies, and inspire a whole town, even its old men, with infamous desires; a father of a family prostitutes his two daughters to save the honour of the two angels; a town is changed into a lake of fire; a woman is transformed into a salt statue; two girls deceive and intoxicate their father in order to commit incest with him, lest, they say, their race should perish, while they have all the inhabitants of the town of Zoar to choose from! All these events, taken together, make up a revolting picture. But if we are reasonable we shall agree with St. Clement of Alexandria and the fathers who have followed him that the whole is allegorical.

Let us remember that that was the way of writing in the East. Parables were so constantly used that even the author of all truth spoke to the Jews only in parables when he came on earth.

Parables make up the whole of the profane theology of antiquity. Saturn devouring his children is evidently time destroying its own works. Minerva is wisdom; she is formed in the head of the master of the gods. The arrows and bandage of Cupid are obvious figures. The fall of Phaëthon is an admirable symbol of ambition. All is not allegory, either in the pagan theology or in the sacred history of the Jewish people. The fathers distinguish between what is

[1] Ninety years old (*Genesis* xvii. 17).—J. M.

purely historical and purely parabolical, and what partakes of the nature of each. It is, I grant, difficult to walk on these slippery paths; but if we walk in the way of virtue, why need we concern ourselves about that of science?

The crime that God punishes here is horrible; let that suffice us. Lot's wife was changed into a salt statue for looking behind her. Let us curb the impulses of curiosity; in a word, let the stores of Holy Writ serve to make us better, if they do not make us more enlightened.

There are, it seems to me, my brethren, two kinds of figurative and mystic interpretation of the Scriptures. The first, and incomparably the better, is to gather from all facts counsels for the conduct of life. If Jacob cruelly wrongs his brother Esau and deceives his father-in-law Laban, let us keep peace in our families and act justly towards our relatives. If the patriarch Reuben dishonours his father's bed, let us regard the incest with horror. If the patriarch Judah commits a still more odious incest with his daughter-in-law Thamar, let us all the more detest these iniquities. When David ravishes the wife of Uriah, and has the husband slain; when Solomon murders his brother; when we find that nearly all the petty kings of the Jews are murderous barbarians, let us mend our ways as we read this awful list of crimes. Let us read the whole Bible in this spirit. It discomposes the man who would be learned; it consoles the man who is content to be good.

The other way to detect the hidden meaning of the Scriptures is to regard each event as an historical and physical emblem. That was the method followed by St. Clement, the great Origen, the respectable St. Augustine, and so many other fathers. According to them, the piece of red cloth which the harlot Rahab hung from her window is the blood of Jesus Christ. Moses spreading out his arms foreshadows the sign of the cross. Judah tying his ass to a vine prefigures the entrance of Christ into Jerusalem. St. Augustine compares the ark of Noah to Jesus. St. Ambrose, in the seventh book of his *De Arca*, says that the making of the little door in the side of the ark signifies, or may be regarded as signifying, a part of the human body. Even if all these interpretations were true, what profit should we derive from them? Will men be juster from knowing what the little door of the ark means? This way of interpreting the Holy Scripture is but a subtlety of the mind, and it may injure the innocence of the heart.

Let us set aside all the subjects of contention which divide nations, and fill ourselves with the sentiments which unite them. Submission to God, resignation, justice, kindness, compassion, and tolerance—those are the great principles. May all the theologians of the earth live together as men of business do. Asking not of what country a man is, nor in what practices he was reared, they observe towards each other the inviolable rules of equity, fidelity, and mutual confidence; and by these principles they bind nations together. But those who know only their own opinions, and condemn all others; those who think that the light shines for them alone, and all other men walk in darkness; those who scruple to communicate with foreign religions, should surely be entitled enemies of the human race.

I will not conceal from you that the most learned men affirm that the Pentateuch was not written by Moses. The great Newton, who alone discovered the first principle of nature and the nature of light, the astounding genius who penetrated so deep into ancient history, attributes the Pentateuch to Samuel. Other distinguished scholars think that it was written in the time of Osias by the scribe Saphan; others believe that Esdras wrote it, on returning from the Captivity. All are agreed, together with certain modern Jews, that the work was not written by Moses.

This great objection is not as formidable as it

seems. We assuredly respect the Decalogue, from whatever hand it came. We dispute about the date of several laws which some attribute to Edward III., others to Edward II.; but we do not hesitate to adopt the laws, because we perceive that they are just and useful. Even if those statements in the preamble that are called in question are rejected, we do not reject the law.

Let us always distinguish between dogma and history, and between dogma and that eternal morality which all legislators have taught and all peoples received.

O holy morality! O God who has created it! I will not confine you within the bounds of a province. You reign over all thinking and sentient beings. You are the God of Jacob; but you are the God of the universe.

I cannot end this discourse, my dear brethren, without speaking to you of the prophets. This is one of the large subjects on which our enemies think to confound us. They say that in ancient times every people had its prophets, diviners, or seers. But does it follow that because the Egyptians, for instance, formerly had false prophets the Jews may not have had true prophets? It is said that they had no mission, no rank, no legal authorisation. That is true; but may they not have been authorised by God? They anathematised each other, and treated each other as rogues and fools; the prophet Zedekiah even dared to strike the prophet Michah in the presence of King Josaphat. We do not deny it; the Paralipomena record the fact. But is a ministry less holy because the ministers disgrace it? Have not our priests done things a hundred times worse than the giving of blows?

The commandments of God to the prophets Ezekiel and Hosea scandalise those who think themselves wise. Will they not be wiser if they see that these are allegories, types, parables, in accordance with the ways of the Israelites? And that we have no more right to ask of God an account of the orders he gives in accordance with these ways than to ask the people why they have them? No doubt God could not order a prophet to commit debauch and adultery; but he wished to let us see that he disapproved the crimes and adulteries of his chosen people. If we did not read the Bible in this spirit, we should, alas, be filled with horror and indignation at every page.

Let us find edification in what scandalises others; let us find wholesome food in their poison. When the proper and literal meaning of a passage seems to be in accord with reason, let us keep to it. When it seems to be contrary to the truth or to sound morals, let us seek a hidden meaning that may reconcile truth and sound morals with Holy Scripture. Thus have all the fathers of the Church proceeded; thus do we proceed daily in the commerce of life. We always interpret favourably the discourses of our friends and partisans. Would we treat more harshly the sacred books of the Jews, which are the object of our faith? Let us, in fine, read the Jews' books that we may be Christians; and if they make us not more wise, let them at least make us better.

HOMILY ON THE INTERPRETATION OF THE NEW TESTAMENT

My Brethren,

There are in the New Testament, as there are in the Old, depths that we cannot sound, and sublimities that our poor reason can never attain. I do not propose here either to reconcile the gospels, which seem to contradict each other at times, or to explain mysteries which, by the very fact that they are mysteries, must be inexplicable. Let those who are more learned than I discuss whether the Holy Family betook itself to Egypt after the massacre of the children at Bethlehem, as Matthew says, or remained in Judæa, as Luke says; let them seek if the father of Joseph was named Jacob, his grandfather Matthan, and his great-grandfather Eleazar, or if his great-grandfather was Levi, his grandfather Matthat, and his father Heli. Let them settle this genealogical tree according to their light; it is a study that I respect. I know not if it would enlighten my mind, but I do know that it cannot speak to my heart. Paul the Apostle tells us himself, in his first epistle to Timothy, that we must not trouble ourselves about genealogies. We will not be any the better for knowing precisely who were the ancestors of Joseph, in what year Jesus was born, and whether James was his brother or his cousin. What will it profit us to consult what remains of the Roman annals to see if Augustus really did order a census of all the peoples of the earth when Mary was pregnant with Jesus, Quirinus governor of Syria, and Herod king of Judæa? Quirinus, whom Luke calls Cyrenius, was (the learned say) not governor in the time of Herod, but of Archelaus, ten years later; and Augustus never ordered a census of the Roman Empire.

We are told that the *Epistle to the Hebrews*, attributed to Paul, was not written by Paul; that neither *Revelation* nor the *Gospel of John* was written by John; that the first chapter of this gospel was evidently written by a Greek Platonist; that the book could not possibly come from a Jew; and that no Jew could ever have made Jesus say : " I give you a new commandment : that you love each other." This commandment, they say, was certainly not new. It is given expressly, and in even stronger terms, in the laws of *Leviticus* : " Thou shalt love thy God above all things, and thy neighbour as thyself." Such a man as Jesus Christ—a man learned in the law, who confounded the doctors at the age of twelve, and was ever speaking of the law—could not be ignorant of the law; and his beloved disciple could not possibly have charged him with so palpable a mistake.

Let us not be troubled, my brethren. Let us remember that Jesus spoke a dialect, half Syrian and half Phœnician, that was hardly intelligible to Greeks; that we have the gospel of John only in Greek; that this gospel was written more than fifty years after the death of Jesus; that the copyists may easily have altered the text; and that it is more probable that the text ran, " I give you a commandment that is not new," than that it said : " I give you a new commandment." Let us return to our great principle. The precept is good; it is our duty to fulfil it as well as we may, whether or no Zoroaster was the first to announce it, and Moses copied it, and Jesus renewed it.

Shall we penetrate into the thickest darkness of antiquity to learn whether the darkness which covered the whole earth at the death of Jesus was due to an eclipse of the sun at a time of full moon, whether an astronomer named Phlegon, whom we have no longer, spoke of this phenomenon, or if any one ever saw the star of the three wise men? These are difficulties that may very well interest an antiquarian; but he will not have spent in good works the precious time he devotes to the clearing-up of this chaos; and he will end with more doubt than piety. My brethren, the man who shares his bread with the poor is better than he who has compared the Hebrew text with the Greek, and both of them with the Samaritan.

All that relates to history only gives rise to a thousand disputes; what concerns our duties gives rise to none. You will never understand how the devil took God into the desert; how he tempted him for forty days; or how he carried him to the top of a hill from which he could see all the kingdoms of the world. The devil offering all these things to God will greatly shock you. You will seek the mystery that is hidden in these things, and so many others, and your mind will be fatigued in vain. Every word will plunge you into uncertainty, and the anguish of a restless curiosity which can never be satisfied. But if you confine your attention to morals the storm will pass, and you will rest in the bosom of virtue.

I venture to flatter myself, my brethren, that if the greatest enemies of the Christian religion were to listen to us in this secluded temple, in which the love of virtue brings us together; if Lord Herbert, Lord Shaftesbury, Lord Bolingbroke, Tindal, Toland, Collins, Whiston, Trenchard, Gordon, and Swift were to witness our gentle and innocent simplicity, they would have less disdain and repugnance for us. They cease not to reproach us with an absurd fanaticism. We are not fanatical in belonging to the religion of Jesus. He worshipped one God, as we do; he despised empty ceremonies, as we do. No gospel has said that his mother was the mother of God, or that he was consubstantial with God. In no gospel will you find that the disciples of Jesus should arrogate the title of " Holy Father," or " My Lord," or that a priest who lives at Lambeth should have an income of two thousand a year while so many useful tillers of the soil have hardly the seed for the three or four acres they water with their tears. The gospel did not say to the bishops of Rome : Forge a donation of Constantine in order to seize the city of the Scipios and Cæsars and become sovereigns of Naples. It did not urge the bishops of Germany to profit by a time of anarchy to invade half of Germany. Jesus was a poor man preaching to the poor. What should we say of the followers of Penn and Fox, those enemies of pomp and friends of peace, if they bore golden mitres on their heads and were surrounded by soldiers ; if they grasped the substance of the peoples ; if they would give orders to kings ; if their satellites, with executioners in their train, were to cry out at the top of their voices, " Foolish nations, believe in Fox and Penn, or you will die in torment " ?

You know better than I what a fatal contrast the ages have witnessed between the humility of Jesus and the pride of those who have assumed his name ; between their avarice and his poverty, their debauches and his chastity, his submissiveness and their bloody tyranny.

I confess, my brethren, that no word of his has made such an impression on me as that which he spoke to those who were so brutal as to strike him before he was led to execution : " If I have spoken well, why do you strike me ? " That is what ought to be said to all persecutors. If my opinion differs from yours on things that it is impossible to understand ; if I see the mercy of God where you would see only his power ; if I have said that all the disciples of Jesus were equal, while you have thought it your duty to trample on them ; if I have worshipped God alone while you have given him associates ; if I have spoken ill in differing from you, bear witness of the

evil; and if I have spoken well, why do you heap
on me your insults and epithets? Why do you persecute me, cast me in irons, deliver me to torture
and flames, and insult me even after my death? If,
indeed, I had spoken ill, it was yours only to pity
and instruct me. You are confident that you are
infallible, that your opinion is divine, that the gates of
hell will never prevail against it, that the whole world
will one day embrace your opinion, that the world will
be subject to you, and that you will rule from Mount
Atlas to the islands of Japan. How, then, can my
opinion hurt you? You do not fear me, and you persecute me! You despise me, and do away with me!

What reply can we make, my brethren, to these
modest and forceful reproaches? Only the reply of
the wolf to the lamb, " You have disturbed the water
that I drink." Thus have men treated each other—
the gospel in one hand and sword in the other;
preaching disinterestedness and accumulating treasures, praising humility and walking on the heads
of prostrate princes, recommending mercy and
shedding human blood.

If these barbarians find in the gospel any parable
that may be distorted in their favour by fraudulent
interpretation, they fasten upon it as an anvil on
which they may forge their murderous weapons.

Is there a word about two swords hung above a
wall? They arm themselves at once with a hundred
swords. It is said that a king has killed his fatted
beasts, compelled the blind and the lame to come to
his feast, and cast into outer darkness him who had
no wedding garment; is that, my brethren, a reason
that justifies them in putting you in prison like this
guest, tearing your limbs asunder on the rack, pluck-
ing out your eyes to make you blind like those who
were dragged to the feast, or slaying you as the king
slew his fatted beasts? Yet it is to such equivocal
passages that men have so often appealed for the
right to desolate a large part of the earth.

Those terrible words, "Not peace, but a sword, I bring unto you," have caused more Christians to perish than ambition has ever sacrificed.

The scattered and unhappy Jews are consoled in their wretchedness when they see us always fighting each other from the earliest days of Christianity, always at war in public or in secret, persecuted or persecuting, oppressed or oppressing. They are united, and they laugh at our interminable quarrels. It seems that we have been concerned only in avenging them.

Wretches that we are, we insult the pagans, yet they never knew our theological quarrels; they have never shed a drop of blood for the interpretation of a dogma, and we have flooded the earth with it. In the bitterness of my heart I say to you: Jesus was persecuted, and whoever shares his thoughts will be persecuted. What was Jesus in the eyes of men, who could assuredly have no suspicion of his divinity? A good man who, having been born in poverty, spoke to the poor in opposition to the superstitions of the rich Pharisees and the insolent priests—the Socrates of Galilee. You know how he said to these Pharisees, "Woe unto you, ye blind guides, which strain at a gnat and swallow a camel! Woe unto you, for ye make clean the outside of the cup and of the platter, but within you are full of extortion and excess" (*Matthew* xxiii.).

He often calls them "whitened sepulchres" and "race of vipers." They were, nevertheless, men of some dignity, and they avenged themselves by his death. Arnold of Brescia, John Huss, and Jerome of Prague said much less than this to the pontiffs of their time, and they, too, were put to death. Never tilt against the ruling superstition, unless you be powerful enough to withstand it, or clever enough to escape its pursuit. The fable of Our Lady of Loretto is more extravagant than all Ovid's metamorphoses, it is true; the miracle of St. Januarius at Naples is more ridiculous than the miracle of Egnatia, mentioned by Horace, I agree. But say aloud at Naples or Loretto what you think of these absurdities, and it will cost you your life. It is not so among certain enlightened nations. There the people have their errors, though they are less gross; and the least superstitious people are always the most tolerant.

Cast off all superstition, and be more humane. But when you speak against fanaticism, anger not the fanatics; they are delirious invalids, who would assault their physicians. Let us make their ways more gentle, not aggravate them. And let us instil, drop by drop, into their souls that divine balm of tolerance which they would reject with horror if offered to them in full.

A TREATISE ON TOLERATION

IN CONNECTION WITH THE DEATH OF JEAN CALAS

SHORT ACCOUNT OF THE DEATH OF JEAN CALAS

THE murder of Calas, which was perpetrated with the sword of justice at Toulouse on March 9, 1762, is one of the most singular events that deserve the attention of our own and of later ages. We quickly forget the long lists of the dead who have perished in our battles. It is the inevitable fate of war; those who die by the sword might themselves have inflicted death on their enemies, and did not die without the means of defending themselves. When the risk and the advantage are equal astonishment ceases, and even pity is enfeebled. But when an innocent father is given into the hands of error, of passion, or of fanaticism; when the accused has no defence but his virtue; when those who dispose of his life run no risk but that of making a mistake; when they can slay with impunity by a legal decree —then the voice of the general public is heard, and each fears for himself. They see that no man's life is safe before a court that has been set up to guard the welfare of citizens, and every voice is raised in a demand of vengeance.

In this strange incident we have to deal with religion, suicide, and parricide. The question was, Whether a father and mother had strangled their son to please God, a brother had strangled his brother, and a friend had strangled his friend; or whether the judges had incurred the reproach of breaking on the wheel an innocent father, or of sparing a guilty mother, brother, and friend.

Jean Calas, a man of sixty-eight years, had been engaged in commerce at Toulouse for more than forty years, and was recognised by all who knew him as a good father.   He was a Protestant, as were also his wife and family, except one son, who had abjured the heresy, and was in receipt of a small allowance from his father.   He seemed to be so far removed from the absurd fanaticism that breaks the bonds of society that he had approved the conversion of his son [Louis Calas], and had had in his service for thirty years a zealous Catholic woman, who had reared all his children.

One of the sons of Jean Calas, named Marc Antoine, was a man of letters.   He was regarded as of a restless, sombre, and violent character.   This young man, failing to enter the commercial world, for which he was unfitted, or the legal world, because he could not obtain the necessary certificate that he was a Catholic, determined to end his life, and informed a friend of his intention.   He strengthened his resolution by reading all that has ever been written on suicide.

Having one day lost his money in gambling, he determined to carry out his plan on that very day. A personal friend and friend of the family, named Lavaisse, a young man of nineteen, well known for his candid and kindly ways, the son of a distinguished lawyer at Toulouse, had come from Bordeaux on the previous day, October 12, 1761.   He happened to sup with the Calas family.   The father, mother, Marc Antoine, the elder son, and Pierre, the second son, were present.   After supper they withdrew to a small room.   Marc Antoine disappeared, and when young Lavaisse was ready to go, and he and Pierre Calas had gone downstairs, they found, near the shop below, Marc Antoine in his shirt, hanging from a door, his coat folded under the counter.   His shirt

was unruffled, his hair was neatly combed, and he
had no wound or mark on the body.

We will omit the details which were given in
court, and the grief and despair of his parents; their
cries were heard by the neighbours. Lavaisse and
Pierre, beside themselves, ran for surgeons and the
police.

While they were doing this, and the father and
mother sobbed and wept, the people of Toulouse
gathered round the house. They are superstitious
and impulsive people; they regard as monsters their
brothers who do not share their religion. It was at
Toulouse that solemn thanks were offered to God
for the death of Henry III., and that an oath was
taken to kill any man who should propose to recognise the great and good Henry IV. This city still
celebrates every year, by a procession and fireworks,
the day on which it massacred four thousand heretical
citizens two hundred years ago. Six decrees of the
Council have been passed in vain for the suppression
of this odious festival; the people of Toulouse
celebrate it still like a floral festival.[1]

Some fanatic in the crowd cried out that Jean
Calas had hanged his son Marc Antoine. The cry
was soon repeated on all sides; some adding that the
deceased was to have abjured Protestantism on the
following day, and that the family and young Lavaisse
had strangled him out of hatred of the Catholic religion. In a moment all doubt had disappeared.
The whole town was persuaded that it is a point of
religion with the Protestants for a father and mother

[1] The condition of Toulouse will be best understood from
a description of these processions which Voltaire gives elsewhere. In front walked the shoemakers, bearing the authentic
head of a prince of Peloponnesus, who had been Bishop of
Toulouse *during the lifetime* of Christ. After them came the
slaters, carrying the bones of the fourteen thousand children
slain by Herod; the old-clothes dealers, with a piece of the
dress of the Virgin Mary; and the tailors, with the relics of
St. Peter and St. Paul.—J. M.

to kill their children when they wish to change their faith.

The agitation could not end here. It was imagined that the Protestants of Languedoc had held a meeting the night before; that they had, by a majority of votes, chosen an executioner for the sect; that the choice had fallen on young Lavaisse; and that, in the space of twenty-four hours, the young man had received the news of his appointment, and had come from Bordeaux to help Jean Calas, his wife, and their son Pierre to strangle a friend, son, and brother.

The captain of Toulouse, David, excited by these rumours and wishing to give effect to them by a prompt execution, took a step which is against the laws and regulations. He put the Calas family, the Catholic servant, and Lavaisse in irons.

A report not less vicious than his procedure was published. He even went farther. Marc Antoine Calas had died a Calvinist; and, if he had taken his own life, his body was supposed to be dragged on a hurdle. Instead of this, he was buried with great pomp in the church of St. Stephen, although the priest protested against this profanation.

There are in Languedoc four confraternities of penitents—the white, the blue, the grey, and the black. Their members wear a long hood, with a cloth mask, pierced with two holes for the eyes. They endeavoured to induce the Duke of Fitz-James, the governor of the province, to enter their ranks, but he refused. The white penitents held a solemn service over Marc Antoine Calas, as over a martyr. No church ever celebrated the feast of a martyr with more pomp; but it was a terrible pomp. They had raised above a magnificent bier a skeleton, which was made to move its bones. It represented Marc Antoine Calas holding a palm in one hand, and in the other the pen with which he was to sign his abjuration of heresy. This pen, in point of fact, signed the death-sentence of his father.

The only thing that remained for the poor devil

who had taken his life was canonisation. Everybody regarded him as a saint; some invoked him, others went to pray at his tomb, others sought miracles of him, and others, again, related the miracles he had wrought. A monk extracted some of his teeth, to have permanent relics of him. A pious woman, who was rather deaf, told how she heard the sound of bells. An apoplectic priest was cured, after taking an emetic. Legal declarations of these prodigies were drawn up. The writer of this account has in his possession the attestation that a young man of Toulouse went mad because he had prayed for several nights at the tomb of the new saint, and could not obtain the miracle he sought.

Some of the magistrates belonged to the confraternity of white penitents. From that moment the death of Jean Calas seemed inevitable.

What contributed most to his fate was the approach of that singular festival which the people of Toulouse hold every year in memory of the massacre of four thousand Huguenots. The year 1762 was the bicentenary of the event. The city was decorated with all the trappings of the ceremony, and the heated imagination of the people was still further excited. It was stated publicly that the scaffold on which the Calas were to be executed would be the chief ornament of the festival; it was said that Providence itself provided these victims for sacrifice in honour of our holy religion. A score of people heard these, and even more violent things. And this in our days—in an age when philosophy has made so much progress, and a hundred academies are writing for the improvement of our morals! It would seem that fanaticism is angry at the success of reason, and combats it more furiously.

Thirteen judges met daily to bring the trial to a close. There was not, and could not be, any evidence against the family; but a deluded religion took the place of proof. Six of the judges long persisted in con-

demning Jean Calas, his son, and Lavaisse to the
wheel, and the wife of Jean Calas to the stake.   The
other seven, more moderate, wished at least to make
an inquiry.   The discussions were long and frequent.
One of the judges, convinced that the accused were
innocent and the crime was impossible, spoke strongly
on their behalf.   He opposed a zeal for humanity to
the zeal for severity, and became the public pleader
for the Calas in Toulouse, where the incessant cries
of outraged religion demanded the blood of the
accused.   Another judge, known for his violent
temper, spoke against the Calas with the same spirit.
At last, amid great excitement, they both threw up
the case and retired to the country.

But by a singular misfortune the judge who was
favourable to the Calas had the delicacy to persist
in his resignation, and the other returned to condemn those whom he could not judge.   His voice it
was that drew up the condemnation to the wheel.
There were now eight votes to five, as one of the six
opposing judges had passed to the more severe party
after considerable discussion.

It seems that in a case of parricide, when a father
is to be condemned to the most frightful death, the
verdict ought to be unanimous, as the evidence for
so rare a crime ought to be such as to convince
everybody.[1]   The slightest doubt in such a case

---

[1] I know only two instances in history of fathers being
charged with killing their children on account of religion.
The first is the case of the father of St. Barbara, or Ste. Barbe.
He had had two windows made in his bathroom.   Barbara,
in his absence, had a third made, to honour the Holy Trinity.
She made the sign of the cross on the marble columns *with
the tip of her finger*, and it was deeply engraved on the stone.
Her son came angrily upon her, sword in hand; but she
escaped through a mountain, which opened to receive her.
The father went round the mountain and caught her.   She
was stripped and flogged, but God clothed her in a white
cloud.   In the end her father cut off her head.   So says the
Flower of the Saints.
The second case is that of Prince Hermenegild.   He
rebelled against his father, the king, gave him battle (in

should intimidate a judge who is to sign the death-sentence. The weakness of our reason and its inadequacy are shown daily; and what greater proof of it can we have than when we find a citizen condemned to the wheel by a majority of one vote? In ancient Athens there had to be fifty votes above the half to secure a sentence of death. It shows us, most unprofitably, that the Greeks were wiser and more humane than we.

It seemed impossible that Jean Calas, an old man of sixty-eight years, whose limbs had long been swollen and weak, had been able to strangle and hang a young man in his twenty-eighth year, above the average in strength. It seemed certain that he must have been assisted in the murder by his wife, his son Pierre, Lavaisse, and the servant. They had not left each other's company for an instant on the evening of the fatal event. But this supposition was just as absurd as the other. How could a zealous Catholic servant allow Huguenots to kill a young man, reared by herself, to punish him for embracing her own religion? How could Lavaisse have come expressly from Bordeaux to strangle his friend, whose conversion was unknown to him? How could a tender mother lay hands on her son? How could the whole of them together strangle a young man who was stronger than all of them without a long and violent struggle, without cries that would have aroused the neighbours, without repeated blows and torn garments?

It was evident that, if there had been any crime, all the accused were equally guilty, as they had never left each other for a moment; it was evident that they were not all guilty; and it was evident that the father alone could not have done it. Nevertheless, the father alone was condemned to the wheel.

The reason of the sentence was as inconceivable as

---

584), and was beaten and killed by an officer. As his father was an Arian, he was regarded as a martyr.

all the rest. The judges, who were bent on executing Jean Calas, persuaded the others that the weak old man could not endure the torture, and would on the scaffold confess his crime and accuse his accomplices. They were confounded when the old man, expiring on the wheel, prayed God to witness his innocence, and begged him to pardon his judges.

They were compelled to pass a second sentence in contradiction of the first, and to set free the mother, the son Pierre, the young Lavaisse, and the servant; but one of the councillors pointing out that this verdict gave the lie to the other, that they were condemning themselves, and that, as the accused were all together at the supposed hour of the crime, the acquittal of the survivors necessarily proved the innocence of the dead father, they decided to banish Pierre Calas. This banishment seemed as illogical and absurd as all the rest. Pierre Calas was either guilty or innocent. If he was guilty, he should be broken on the wheel like his father; if he was innocent, they had no right to banish him. However, the judges, terrified by the execution of the father and the touching piety of his end, thought they were saving their honour by affecting to pardon the son, as if it were not a fresh prevarication to pardon him; and they thought that the banishment of this poor and helpless young man was not a great injustice after that they had already committed.

They began with threatening Pierre Calas, in his dungeon, that he would suffer like his father if he did not renounce his religion. The young man attests this on oath: "A Dominican monk came to my cell and threatened me with the same kind of death if I did not give up my religion."

Pierre Calas, on leaving the city, met a priest, who compelled him to return to Toulouse. They confined him in a Dominican convent, and forced him to perform Catholic functions. It was part of what they wanted. It was the price of his father's blood, and religion seemed to be avenged.

The daughters were taken from the mother and put in a convent. The mother, almost sprinkled with the blood of her husband, her eldest son dead, the younger banished, deprived of her daughters and all her property, was alone in the world, without bread, without hope, dying of the intolerable misery. Certain persons, having carefully examined the circumstances of this horrible adventure, were so impressed that they urged the widow, who had retired into solitude, to go and demand justice at the feet of the throne.[1] At the time she shrank from publicity; moreover, being English by birth, and having been transplanted into a French province in early youth, the name of Paris terrified her. She imagined that the capital of the kingdom would be still more barbaric than the capital of Languedoc. At length the duty of clearing the memory of her husband prevailed over her weakness. She reached Paris almost at the point of death. She was astonished at her reception, at the help and the tears that were given to her.[2]

At Paris reason dominates fanaticism, however powerful it be; in the provinces fanaticism almost always overcomes reason.

M. de Beaumont, the famous advocate of the Parlement de Paris, undertook to defend her, and drew up a memorial signed by fifteen other advocates. M. Loiseau, not less eloquent, drew up a memoir on behalf of the family. M. Mariette, an advocate of the Council, drew up a judicial inquiry which brought conviction to every mind. These three generous de-

[1] Voltaire nobly conceals his work. It was he who, from his exile near Geneva, sent for young Calas, made searching inquiries in Toulouse, and instructed the Parisian lawyers to appeal. He enlisted the interest of English and French visitors at Geneva, and there was " a rivalry in generosity between the two nations." After a long struggle with the Toulouse authorities the sentence was reversed at Paris amid general enthusiasm. The king very generously pensioned the widow and the other victims.—J. M.

[2] Thanks to Voltaire and to the progress of Rationalism at Paris, she was received with the greatest enthusiasm and generosity.—J. M.

fenders of the laws of innocence gave to the widow
the profit on the sale of their memoirs. Paris and
the whole of Europe were moved with pity, and
demanded justice for the unfortunate woman. The
verdict was given by the public long before it was
signed by the Council.

The spirit of pity penetrated the ministry, in spite
of the torrent of business that so often shuts out
pity, and in spite of that daily sight of misery that
does even more to harden the heart. The daughters
were restored to their mother. As they sat, clothed
in crape and bathed in tears, their judges were seen
to weep.

They had still enemies, however, for it was a
question of religion. Many of those people who are
known in France as " devout " [1] said openly that
it was much better to let an innocent old Calvinist
be slain than to compel eight Councillors of Languedoc to admit that they were wrong. One even heard
such phrases as " There are more magistrates than
Calas "; and it was inferred that the Calas family
ought to be sacrificed to the honour of the magistrates. They did not reflect that the honour of
judges, like that of other men, consists in repairing
their blunders. It is not believed in France that the
Pope is infallible, even with the assistance of his
cardinals; [2] we might just as well admit that eight
judges of Toulouse are not. All other people, more
reasonable and disinterested, said that the Toulouse
verdict would be reversed all over Europe, even if
special considerations prevented it from being reversed
by the Council.

Such was the position of this astonishing adventure when it moved certain impartial and reasonable
persons to submit to the public a few reflections on

[1] In ancient Rome the *devoti* were those who devoted
themselves to the good of the Republic.

[2] The Catholic Church did not discover the infallibility
of the Pope until 1870, since which date his lips have remained,
officially, closed.—J. M.

the subject of toleration, indulgence, and pity, which the Abbé Houteville calls "a monstrous dogma," in his garbled version of the facts, and which reason calls an "appanage of nature."

Either the judges of Toulouse, swept away by the fanaticism of the people, have broken on the wheel an innocent man, which is unprecedented; or the father and his wife strangled their elder son, with the assistance of another son and a friend, which is unnatural. In either case the abuse of religion has led to a great crime. It is, therefore, of interest to the race to inquire whether religion ought to be charitable or barbaric.

CONSEQUENCES OF THE EXECUTION OF JEAN CALAS

If the white penitents were the cause of the execution of an innocent man, the utter ruin of a family, and the dispersal and humiliation that attach to an execution, though they should punish only injustice; if the haste of the white penitents to commemorate as a saint one who, according to our barbaric customs, should have been dragged on a hurdle, led to the execution of a virtuous parent; they ought indeed to be penitents for the rest of their lives. They and the judges should weep, but not in a long white robe, and with no mask to hide their tears.

We respect all confraternities; they are edifying. But can whatever good they may do the State outweigh this appalling evil that they have done? It seems that they have been established by the zeal which in Languedoc fires the Catholics against those whom we call Huguenots. One would say that they had taken vows to hate their brothers; for we have religion enough left to hate and to persecute, and we have enough to love and to help. What would happen if these confraternities were controlled by enthusiasts, as were once certain congregations of artisans and "gentlemen," among whom, as one of our most eloquent and learned magistrates said, the seeing of visions was reduced to a fine art?   What would happen if these confraternities set up again those dark chambers, called "meditation rooms," on which were painted devils armed with horns and claws, gulfs of flame, crosses and daggers, with the holy name of Jesus surmounting the picture? [1] What a spectacle for eyes that are already fascinated, and imaginations that are as inflamed as they are submissive to their confessors !

There have been times when, as we know only too well, confraternities were dangerous.   The Fratelli and the Flagellants gave trouble enough.   The League [2] began with associations of that kind.   Why should they distinguish themselves thus from other citizens?   Did they think themselves more perfect? The very claim is an insult to the rest of the nation. Did they wish all Christians to enter their confraternity?   What a sight it would be to have all Europe in hoods and masks, with two little round holes in front of the eyes !   Do they seriously think that God prefers this costume to that of ordinary folk?   Further, this garment is the uniform of controversialists, warning their opponents to get to arms.   It may excite a kind of civil war of minds, and would perhaps end in fatal excesses, unless the king and his ministers were as wise as the fanatics were demented.

We know well what the price has been ever since Christians began to dispute about dogmas.   Blood has flowed, on scaffolds and in battles, from the fourth century to our own days.[3]   We will restrict ourselves here to the wars and horrors which the Reformation struggle caused, and see what was the

[1] A thrust at the Jesuits.—J. M.

[2] The Catholic League for the suppression of Protestantism in France, in the second half of the sixteenth century, led to much war and bloodshed.—J. M.

[3] In his treatise *Dieu et les Hommes* Voltaire, after a very incomplete survey of history, puts the number of victims of religious wars and quarrels at 9,468,800.—J. M.

source of them in France. Possibly a short and faithful account of those calamities will open the eyes of the uninformed and touch the hearts of the humane.

THE IDEA OF THE REFORMATION

When enlightenment spread, with the renaissance of letters in the fifteenth century, there was a very general complaint of abuses, and everybody agrees that the complaint was just.

Pope Alexander VI. had openly bought the papal tiara, and his five bastards shared its advantages. His son, the cardinal-duke of Borgia, made an end, in concert with his father, of Vitelli, Urbino, Gravina, Oliveretto, and a hundred other nobles, in order to seize their lands. Julius II., animated by the same spirit, excommunicated Louis XII. and gave his kingdom to the first occupant; while he himself, helmet on head and cuirass on back, spread blood and fire over part of Italy. Leo X., to pay for his pleasures, sold indulgences, as the taxes are sold in the open market. They·who revolted against this brigandage were, at least, not wrong from the moral point of view. Let us see if they were wrong in politics.

They said that, since Jesus Christ had never exacted fees, nor sold dispensations for this world or indulgences for the next, one might refuse to pay a foreign prince the price of these things. Supposing that our fees to Rome and the dispensations which we still buy [1] did not cost us more than five hundred thousand francs a year, it is clear that, since the time of Francis I., we should have paid, in two hundred and fifty years, a hundred and twenty million francs; allowing for the change of value in money, we may say about two hundred and fifty millions [£10,000,000]. One may, therefore, without blasphemy, admit that the heretics, in proposing to abolish these singular taxes, which will astonish a

[1] To marry within certain degrees of kindred, etc.—J. M.

later age, did not do a very grave wrong to the kingdom, and that they were rather good financiers than
bad subjects. Let us add that they alone knew
Greek, and were acquainted with antiquity. Let us
grant that, in spite of their errors, we owe to them
the development of the human mind, so long buried
in the densest barbarism.

But, as they denied the existence of Purgatory,
which it is not permitted to doubt, and which brought
a considerable income to the monks; and as they
did not venerate relics, which ought to be venerated,
and which are a source of even greater profit—in
fine, as they assailed much-respected dogmas, the
only answer to them at first was to burn them. The
king, who protected and subsidised them in Germany,
walked at the head of a procession in Paris, and at
the close a number of the wretches were executed.
This was the manner of execution. They were hung
at the end of a long beam, which was balanced, like
a see-saw, across a tree. A big fire was lit under-
neath, and they were alternately sunk into it and
raised out. Their torments were thus protracted,
until death relieved them from a more hideous
punishment than any barbarian had ever invented.

Shortly before the death of Francis I. certain
members of the Parlement de Provence, instigated
by their clergy against the inhabitants of Merindol
and Cabrières, asked the king for troops to support
the execution of nineteen persons of the district
whom they had condemned. They had six thousand
slain, without regard to sex or age or infancy, and
they reduced thirty towns to ashes. These people,
who had not hitherto been heard of, were, no doubt,
in the wrong to have been born Waldensians; but
that was their only crime. They had been settled
for three hundred years in the deserts and on the
mountains, which they had, with incredible labour,
made fertile. Their quiet, pastoral life represented
the supposed innocence of the first ages of men.
They knew the neighbouring towns only by selling

fruit to them. They had no law-courts and never warred; they did not defend themselves. They were slain as one slays animals in an enclosure.

After the death of Francis I.—a prince who is better known for his amours and misfortunes than his cruelty—the execution of a thousand heretics, especially of the Councillor of the Parlement, Dubourg, and the massacre of Vassy, caused the persecuted sect to take to arms. They had increased in the light of the flames and under the sword of the executioner, and substituted fury for patience. They imitated the cruelties of their enemies. Nine civil wars filled France with carnage; and a peace more fatal than war led to the massacre of St. Bartholomew, which is without precedent in the annals of crime.

The [Catholic] League assassinated Henry III. and Henry IV. by the hands of a Dominican monk, and of a monster who had belonged to the order of St. Bernard. There are those who say that humanity, indulgence, and liberty of conscience are horrible things. Candidly, could they have brought about calamities such as these?

WHETHER TOLERATION IS DANGEROUS, AND AMONG WHAT PEOPLES IT IS FOUND

There are some who say that, if we treated with paternal indulgence those erring brethren who pray to God in bad French [instead of bad Latin], we should be putting weapons in their hands, and would once more witness the battles of Jarnac, Moncontour, Coutras, Dreux, and St. Denis. I do not know anything about this, as I am not a prophet; but it seems to me an illogical piece of reasoning to say: " These men rebelled when I treated them ill, therefore they will rebel when I treat them well."

I would venture to take the liberty to invite those who are at the head of the government, and those who are destined for high positions, to reflect carefully whether one really has ground to fear that kindness will lead to the same revolts as cruelty;

whether what happened in certain circumstances is sure to happen in different circumstances; if the times, public opinion, and morals are unchanged.

The Huguenots, it is true, have been as inebriated with fanaticism and stained with blood as we. But are this generation as barbaric as their fathers? Have not time, the progress of reason, good books, and the humanising influence of society had an effect on the leaders of these people? And do we not perceive that the aspect of nearly the whole of Europe has been changed within the last fifty years?

Government is stronger everywhere, and morals have improved. The ordinary police, supported by numerous standing armies, gives us some security against a return to that age of anarchy in which Calvinistic peasants fought Catholic peasants, hastily enrolled between the sowing and the harvest.

Different times have different needs. It would be absurd to decimate the Sorbonne to-day because it once presented a demand for the burning of the Maid of Orleans, declared that Henry III. had forfeited his kingdom, excommunicated him, and proscribed the great Henry IV. We will not think of inquiring into the other bodies in the kingdom who committed the same excesses in those frenzied days. It would not only be unjust, but would be as stupid as to purge all the inhabitants of Marseilles because they had the plague in 1720.

Shall we go and sack Rome, as the troops of Charles V. did, because Sixtus V. in 1585 granted an indulgence of nine years to all Frenchmen who would take up arms against their sovereign? Is it not enough to prevent Rome for ever from reverting to such excesses?

The rage that is inspired by the dogmatic spirit and the abuse of the Christian religion, wrongly conceived, has shed as much blood and led to as many disasters in Germany, England, and even Holland, as in France. Yet religious difference causes no trouble to-day in those States.   The Jew, the Catholic, the Greek, the Lutheran, the Calvinist, the Anabaptist, the Socinian, the Memnonist, the Moravian, and so many others, live like brothers in these countries, and contribute alike to the good of the social body.

They fear no longer in Holland that disputes about predestination will end in heads being cut off. They fear no longer at London that the quarrels of Presbyterians and Episcopalians about liturgies and surplices will lead to the death of a king on the scaffold.   A populous and wealthier Ireland will no longer see its Catholic citizens sacrifice its Protestant citizens to God during two months, bury them alive, hang their mothers to gibbets, tie the girls to the necks of their mothers, and see them expire together; or put swords in the hands of their prisoners and guide their hands to the bosoms of their wives, their fathers, their mothers, and their daughters, thinking to make parricides of them, and damn them as well as exterminate them.[1]   Such is the account given by Rapin Thoyras, an officer in Ireland, and almost a contemporary; so we find in all the annals and histories of England.   It will never be repeated. Philosophy, the sister of religion, has disarmed the hands that superstition had so long stained with blood; and the human mind, awakening from its intoxication, is amazed at the excesses into which fanaticism had led it.

We have in France a rich province in which the Lutherans outnumber the Catholics.   The University of Alsace is in the hands of the Lutherans.   They occupy some of the municipal offices; yet not the least religious quarrel has disturbed this province since it came into the possession of our kings.   Why? Because no one has ever been persecuted in it.   Seek not to vex the hearts of men, and they are yours.

I do not say that all who are not of the same

[1] An exaggerated account of the Ulster rebellion.—J. M.

religion as the prince should share the positions and honours of those who follow the dominant religion. In England the Catholics, who are regarded as attached to the party of the Pretender, are not admitted to office. They even pay double taxes. In other respects, however, they have all the rights of citizens.

Some of the French bishops have been suspected of holding that it redounds neither to their honour nor their profit to have Calvinists in their dioceses. This is said to be one of the greatest obstacles to toleration. I cannot believe it. The episcopal body in France is composed of gentlemen, who think and act with the nobility that befits their birth. They are charitable and generous; so much justice must be done them. They must think that their fugitive subjects will assuredly not be converted in foreign countries, and that, when they return to their pastors, they may be enlightened by their instructions and touched by their example. There would be honour in converting them, and their material interests would not suffer. The more citizens there were, the larger would be the income from the prelate's estates.

A Polish bishop had an Anabaptist for farmer and a Socinian for steward. It was suggested that he ought to discharge and prosecute the latter because he did not believe in consubstantiality, and the former because he did not baptise his child until it was fifteen years old. He replied that they would be damned for ever in the next world, but that they were very useful to him in this.

Let us get out of our grooves and study the rest of the globe. The Sultan governs in peace twenty million people of different religions; two hundred thousand Greeks live in security at Constantinople; the *muphti* himself nominates and presents to the emperor the Greek patriarch, and they also admit a Latin patriarch. The Sultan nominates Latin bishops for some of the Greek islands, using the following formula : " I command him to go and reside as bishop in the island of Chios, according to their ancient usage and their vain ceremonies." The empire is full of Jacobites, Nestorians, and Monothelites; it contains Copts, Christians of St. John, Jews, and Hindoos. The annals of Turkey do not record any revolt instigated by any of these religions.

Go to India, Persia, or Tartary, and you will find the same toleration and tranquillity. Peter the Great patronised all the cults in his vast empire. Commerce and agriculture profited by it, and the body politic never suffered from it.

The government of China has not, during the four thousand years of its known history, had any cult but the simple worship of one God. Nevertheless, it tolerates the superstitions of Fo, and permits a large number of bonzes, who would be dangerous if the prudence of the courts did not restrain them.

It is true that the great Emperor Yang-Chin, perhaps the wisest and most magnanimous emperor that China ever had, expelled the Jesuits. But it was not because he was intolerant; it was because the Jesuits were. They themselves give, in their curious letters, the words of the good prince to them : " I know that your religion is intolerant; I know what you have done in Manila and Japan. You deceived my father; think not to deceive me." If you read the whole of his speech to them, you will see that he was one of the wisest and most clement of men. How could he retain European physicians who, under pretence of showing thermometers and æolipiles at court, had carried off a prince of the blood? What would he have said if he had read our history and was acquainted with the days of our League and of the Gunpowder Plot?

It was enough for him to be informed of the indecent quarrels of the Jesuits, Dominicans, Franciscans, and secular priests sent into his State from the ends of the earth. They came to preach the truth, and fell to anathematising each other. Hence the Emperor was bound to expel the foreign disturbers. But how kindly he dismissed them ! What paternal care did he not devote to their journey, and in order to protect them from insult on the way ? Their very banishment was a lesson in toleration and humanity.

The Japanese were the most tolerant of all men. A dozen peaceful religions throve in their empire, when the Jesuits came with a thirteenth. As they soon showed that they would tolerate no other, there arose a civil war, even more frightful than that of the League, and the land was desolated. In the end the Christian religion was drowned in blood ; the Japanese closed their empire, and regarded us only as wild beasts, like those which the English have cleared out of their island. The minister Colbert, knowing how we need the Japanese, who have no need of us, tried in vain to reopen commerce with their empire. He found them inflexible.

Thus the whole of our continent shows us that we must neither preach nor practise intolerance.

Turn your eyes to the other hemisphere. Study Carolina, of which the wise Locke was the legislator. Seven fathers of families sufficed to set up a public cult approved by the law ; and this liberty gave rise to no disorder. Heaven preserve us from quoting this as an example for France to follow ! We quote it only to show that the greatest excess of toleration was not followed by the slightest dissension. But what is good and useful in a young colony is not suitable for a long-established kingdom.

What shall we say of the primitive people who have been derisively called Quakers, but who, however ridiculous their customs may be, have been so virtuous and given so useful a lesson of peace to other men ? There are a hundred thousand of them in Pennsylvania. Discord and controversy are unknown in the happy country they have made for themselves ; and the very name of their chief town, Philadelphia, which unceasingly reminds them that all men are brothers, is an example and a shame to nations that are yet ignorant of toleration.

Toleration, in fine, never led to civil war; intolerance has covered the earth with carnage. Choose, then, between these rivals—between the mother who would have her son slain and the mother who yields, provided his life be spared.

I speak here only of the interest of nations. While respecting theology, as I do, I regard in this article only the physical and moral well-being of society. I beg every impartial reader to weigh these truths, verify them, and add to them. Attentive readers, who restrain not their thoughts, always go farther than the author.

HOW TOLERATION MAY BE ADMITTED

I venture to think that some enlightened and magnanimous minister, some humane and wise prelate, some prince who puts his interest in the number of his subjects and his glory in their welfare, may deign to glance at this inartistic and defective paper. He will supply its defects and say to himself: What do I risk in seeing my land cultivated and enriched by a larger number of industrious workers, the revenue increased, the State more flourishing?

Germany would be a desert strewn with the bones of Catholics, Protestants, and Anabaptists, slain by each other, if the peace of Westphalia had not at length brought freedom of conscience.

We have Jews at Bordeaux and Metz and in Alsace; we have Lutherans, Molinists, and Jansenists; can we not suffer and control Calvinists on much the same terms as those on which Catholics are tolerated at London? The more sects there are, the less danger in each. Multiplicity enfeebles them. They are all restrained by just laws which forbid disorderly meetings, insults, and sedition, and are ever enforced by the community.

We know that many fathers of families, who have made large fortunes in foreign lands, are ready to return to their country. They ask only the protection of natural law, the validity of their marriages, security as to the condition of their children, the right to inherit from their fathers, and the enfranchisement of their persons. They ask not for public chapels, or the right to municipal offices and dignities. Catholics have not these things in England and other countries. It is not a question of giving immense privileges and secure positions to a faction, but of allowing a peaceful people to live, and of moderating the laws once, but no longer, necessary. It is not our place to tell the ministry what is to be done; we do but ask consideration for the unfortunate.

How many ways there are of making them useful, and preventing them from ever being dangerous! The prudence of the ministry and the Council, supported as it is by force, will easily discover these means, which are already happily employed by other nations.

There are still fanatics among the Calvinistic populace; but it is certain that there are far more among the convulsionary [bigoted Catholic] populace. The dregs of the fanatical worshippers of St. Medard count as nothing in the nation; the dregs of the Calvinistic prophets are annihilated. The great means to reduce the number of fanatics, if any remain, is to submit that disease of the mind to the treatment of reason, which slowly, but infallibly, enlightens men. Reason is gentle and humane. It inspires liberality, suppresses discord, and strengthens virtue; it has more power to make obedience to the laws attractive than force has to compel it. And shall we take no account of the ridicule that attaches to-day to the enthusiasm of these good people? Ridicule is a strong barrier to the extravagance of all sectarians. The past is as if it had never been. We must always start from the present—from the point which nations have already reached.

There was a time when it was thought necessary to issue decrees against those who taught a doctrine at variance with the categories of Aristotle, the abhorrence of a vacuum, the quiddities, the universal apart from the object. We have in Europe more than a hundred volumes of jurisprudence on sorcery and the way to distinguish between false and real sorcerers. The excommunication of grasshoppers and harmful insects has been much practised, and still survives in certain rituals. But the practice is over; Aristotle and the sorcerers and grasshoppers are left in peace. There are countless instances of this folly, once thought so important. Other follies arise from time to time; but they have their day and are abandoned. What would happen to-day if a man were minded to call himself a Carpocratian, a Eutychian, a Monothelite, Monophysist, a Nestorian, or a Manichæan? We should laugh at him, as at a man dressed in the garb of former days.

The nation was beginning to open its eyes when the Jesuits Le Tellier and Doucin fabricated the bull *Unigenitus* and sent it to Rome. They thought that they still lived in those ignorant times when the most absurd statements were accepted without inquiry. They ventured even to condemn the proposition, a truth of all times and all places: " The fear of unjust excommunication should not prevent one from doing one's duty." It was a proscription of reason, of the liberties of the Gallican Church, and of the fundamental principle of morals. It was to say to men : God commands you never to do your duty if you fear injustice. Never was common-sense more outrageously challenged ! The counsellors of Rome were not on their guard. The papal court was persuaded that the bull was necessary, and that the nation desired it ; it was signed, sealed, and dispatched. You know the result ; assuredly, if they had been foreseen, the bull would have been modified. There were angry quarrels, which the prudence and goodness of the king have settled.

So it is in regard to a number of the points which divide the Protestants and ourselves. Some are of no consequence; some are more serious; but on these points the fury of the controversy has so far abated that the Protestants themselves no longer enter into disputes in their churches.

It is a time of disgust, of satiety, or, rather, of reason, that may be used as an epoch and guarantee of public tranquillity. Controversy is an epidemic disease that nears its end, and what is now needed is gentle treatment. It is to the interest of the State that its expatriated children should return modestly to the homes of their fathers. Humanity demands it, reason counsels it, and politics need not fear it.

WHETHER INTOLERANCE IS OF NATURAL AND HUMAN LAW

Natural law is that indicated to men by nature. You have reared a child; he owes you respect as a father, gratitude as a benefactor. You have a right to the products of the soil that you have cultivated with your own hands. You have given or received a promise; it must be kept.

Human law must in every case be based on natural law. All over the earth the great principle of both is: Do not unto others what you would that they do not unto you. Now, in virtue of this principle, one man cannot say to another: " Believe what I believe, and what thou canst not believe, or thou shalt perish." Thus do men speak in Portugal, Spain, and Goa. In some other countries they are now content to say: " Believe, or I detest thee; believe, or I will do thee all the harm I can. Monster, thou sharest not my religion, and therefore hast no religion; thou shalt be a thing of horror to thy neighbours, thy city, and thy province."

If it were a point of human law to behave thus, the Japanese should detest the Chinese, who should abhor the Siamese; the Siamese, in turn, should persecute the Thibetans, who should fall upon the Hindoos. A Mogul should tear out the heart of the first Malabarian he met; the Malabarian should slay the Persian, who might massacre the Turk; and all of them should fling themselves against the Christians, who have so long devoured each other.

The supposed right of intolerance is absurd and barbaric. It is the right of the tiger; nay, it is far worse, for tigers do but tear in order to have food, while we rend each other for paragraphs.

WHETHER INTOLERANCE WAS KNOWN TO THE GREEKS

The peoples of whom history has given us some slight knowledge regarded their different religions as links that bound them together; it was an association of the human race. There was a kind of right to hospitality among the gods, just as there was among men. When a stranger reached a town, his first act was to worship the gods of the country; even the gods of enemies were strictly venerated. The Trojans offered prayers to the gods who fought for the Greeks.

Alexander, in the deserts of Libya, went to consult the god Ammon, whom the Greeks called Zeus and the Latins Jupiter, though they both had their own Zeus or Jupiter at home. When a town was besieged, sacrifices and prayers were offered to the gods of the town to secure their favour. Thus in the very midst of war religion united men and moderated their fury, though at times it enjoined on them inhuman and horrible deeds.

I may be wrong, but it seems to me that not one of the ancient civilised nations restricted the freedom of thought.[1] Each of them had a religion, but it seems to me that they used it in regard to men as they did in regard to their gods. All of them recognised a

---

[1] This position could be held only in a modified form in regard to ancient Greece. See E. S. P. Haynes's work, *Religious Persecution.*—J. M.

supreme God, but they associated with him a prodigious number of lesser divinities. They had only
one cult, but they permitted numbers of special
systems.

The Greeks, for instance, however religious they
were, allowed the Epicureans to deny providence and
the existence of the soul. I need not speak of the
other sects which all offended against the sound idea
of the creative being, yet were all tolerated.

Socrates, who approached nearest to a knowledge
of the Creator, is said to have paid for it, and died a
martyr to the Deity; he is the only man whom the
Greeks put to death for his opinions. If that was
really the cause of his condemnation, however, it is
not to the credit of intolerance, since they punished
only the man who alone gave glory to God, and
honoured those who held unworthy views of the Deity.
The enemies of toleration would, I think, be ill advised
to quote the odious example of the judges of Socrates.

It is evident, moreover, that he was the victim of a
furious party, angered against him. He had made
irreconcilable enemies of the sophists, orators, and
poets who taught in the schools, and of all the teachers
in charge of the children of distinguished men. He
himself admits, in his discourse given to us by Plato,
that he went from house to house proving to the
teachers that they were ignorant. Such conduct
was hardly worthy of one whom an oracle had declared
to be the wisest of men. A priest and a councillor
of the Five Hundred were put forward to accuse him.
I must confess that I do not know what the precise
accusation was; I find only vagueness in his apology.
He is made to say, in general, that he was accused of
instilling into young men sentiments in opposition to
the religion and government. It is the usual method
of calumniators, but a court would demand accredited
facts and precise charges. Of these there is no trace
in the trial of Socrates. We know only that at first
there were two hundred and twenty votes in his
favour. From this we may infer that the court of the

Five Hundred included two hundred and twenty philosophers; I doubt if so many could be found elsewhere. The majority at length condemned him to drink the hemlock; but let us remember that, when the Athenians returned to their senses, they regarded both the accusers and the judges with horror; that Melitus, the chief author of the sentence, was condemned to death for his injustice; and that the others were banished, and a temple was erected to Socrates. Never was philosophy so much avenged and honoured. The case of Socrates is really the most terrible argument that can be used against intolerance. The Athenians had an altar dedicated to foreign gods—the gods they knew not. Could there be a stronger proof, not merely of their indulgence to all nations, but even of respect for their cults?

A French writer, in attempting to justify the massacre of St. Bartholomew, quotes the war of the Phocæans, known as " the sacred war," as if this war had been inspired by cult, or dogma, or theological argument. Nay, it was a question only of determining to whom a certain field belonged; it is the subject of all wars. Beards of corn are not a symbol of faith; no Greek town ever went to war for opinions. What, indeed, would this gentleman have? Would he have us enter upon a " sacred war "?

WHETHER THE ROMANS WERE TOLERANT

Among the ancient Romans you will not find, from Romulus until the days when the Christians disputed with the priests of the empire, a single man persecuted on account of his opinions. Cicero doubted everything; Lucretius denied everything; yet they incurred not the least reproach. Indeed, licence went so far that Pliny, the naturalist, began his book by saying that there is no god, or that, if there is, it is the sun. Cicero, speaking of the lower regions, says : " There is no old woman so stupid as to believe in them (*Non*

est anus tam excors quæ credat)." Juvenal says :
" Even the children do not believe (*Nec pueri credunt*)."
They sang in the theatre at Rome : " There is nothing
after death, and death is nothing (*Post mortem nihil
est, ipsaque mors nihil*)." We may abhor these
maxims, or, at the most, forgive a people whom the
light of the gospel had not reached ; but we must
conclude that the Romans were very tolerant, since
they did not excite a single murmur.

The great principle of the Senate and people of
Rome was, " Offences against the gods are the
business of the gods (*Deorum offensa diis curæ*)."
They dreamed only of conquering, governing, and
civilising the world. They were our legislators and
our conquerors ; and Cæsar, who gave us roads, laws,
and games, never attempted to compel us to abandon
our druids for him, great pontiff as he was of our
sovereign nation.

The Romans did not profess all cults, or assign public
functions to all, but they permitted all. They had
no material object of worship under Numa, no
pictures or statues ; though they presently erected
statues to " the gods of the great nations," whom
they learned from the Greeks. The law of the Twelve
Tables, *Deos peregrinos ne colunto* [" Foreign gods
shall not be worshipped "], means only that public
cult shall be given only to the superior divinities
approved by the Senate. Isis had a temple at Rome
until Tiberius destroyed it. The Jews were engaged
in commerce there since the time of the Punic war,
and had synagogues there in the days of Augustus.
They kept them almost always, as in modern Rome.
Can there be a clearer proof that toleration was
regarded by the Romans as the most sacred line of the
law of nations.

We are told that, as soon as the Christians appeared,
they were persecuted by the Romans, who persecuted
nobody. It seems to me that the statement is entirely
false, and I need only quote St. Paul himself in
disproof of it. In the *Acts of the Apostles* (xxv. 16)

we read that, when Paul was dragged before the Roman Governor by the Jews in some religious quarrel, Festus said : " It is not the manner of the Romans to deliver any man to die before that he which is accused have the accusers face to face, and have licence to answer for himself." These words are the more remarkable for a Roman magistrate, because he seems to have had nothing but contempt for Paul. Deceived by the false light of his reason, he took Paul for a fool, and said : " Much learning doth make thee mad." He was, therefore, having regard only to the equity of Roman law in giving his protection to a stranger for whom he had no esteem.

Thus the Holy Spirit, in inspiring *Acts*, testifies that the Romans were just, and did not persecute. It was not the Romans who fell upon Paul, but the Jews. St. James, the brother of Jesus, was stoned by the order of a Jewish Sadducee, not of a Roman. The Jews alone stoned St. Stephen; and St. Paul, in holding the cloaks of the executioners, certainly did not act as a Roman citizen.[1]

The first Christians had, no doubt, no cause of quarrel with the Romans; their only enemies were the Jews, from whom they were beginning to separate. We know the fierce hatred that sectarians always have for those who leave the sect. There were probably disturbances in the synagogues at Rome. Suetonius says, in his life of Claudius : " Judæos impulsore Christo assidue tumultuantes Roma expulit." [2] He was wrong in saying that they were instigated by Christ, and was not likely to be well informed in

---

[1] The Jews had no right to inflict death after Judæa had become a Roman province, but the authorities at times overlooked these punishments of blasphemy.

[2] Ch. 25. Voltaire has in this followed ecclesiastical custom. The word in Suetonius is not " Christo," but " Chresto," and therefore the passage reads, in English : " Claudius expelled the Jews from Rome for their constant disturbances at the instigation of Chrestus." As Chrestus was not an uncommon name at Rome, there is no need to apply the passage to Christ in any way.—J. M.

detail about a people so much despised at Rome as the Jews were; but he was not mistaken as to the subject of the quarrels. Suetonius wrote under Hadrian, in the second century, when the Christians were not distinct from the Jews in Roman eyes. His words show that the Romans, instead of oppressing the first Christians, rather coerced the Jews who persecuted them. They wished the Roman synagogue to deal as indulgently with their separated brethren as the Senate did. The banished Jews returned soon afterwards, and even attained high positions, in spite of the laws which excluded them, as Dio Cassius and Ulpian tell us. Is it possible that, after the ruin of Jerusalem, the emperors should lavish honours on the Jews, and persecute, and hand over to the executioner or the beasts, Christians, who were regarded as a Jewish sect?

It is said that Nero persecuted them. Tacitus tells us that they were accused of setting fire to Rome, and were abandoned to the fury of the people. Was that on account of their religious belief? Certainly not. Shall we say that the Chinese who were slain by the Dutch a few years ago in the suburbs of Batavia were sacrificed on account of religion? However much a man may wish to deceive himself, it is impossible to ascribe to intolerance the disaster that befell a few half-Jewish, half-Christian men and women at Rome under Nero.[1]

THE MARTYRS

There were Christian martyrs in later years. It is very difficult to discover the precise grounds on which they were condemned; but I venture to think that none of them were put to death on religious grounds under the earlier Emperors. All religions were tolerated, and there is no reason to suppose that the Romans would seek out and persecute certain

[1] The passage of Tacitus (*Annals*, xv. 44) is very generally rejected as an interpolation.—J. M.

obscure men, with a peculiar cult, at a time when they permitted all other religions.

Titus, Trajan, the Antonines, and Decius were not barbarians. How can we suppose that they deprived the Christians alone of a liberty which the whole empire enjoyed? How could they venture to charge the Christians with their secret mysteries when the mysteries of Isis, Mithra, and the Syrian goddess, all alien to the Roman cult, were freely permitted? There must have been other reasons for persecution. Possibly certain special animosities, supported by reasons of State, led to the shedding of Christian blood.

For instance, when St. Lawrence refused to give to the Roman prefect, Cornelius Secularis, the money of the Christians which he held, the prefect and emperor would naturally be irritated. They did not know that St. Lawrence had distributed the money to the poor, and done a charitable and holy act. They regarded him as rebellious, and had him put to death.[1]

Consider the martyrdom of St. Polyeuctes. Was he condemned on the ground of religion alone? He enters the temple, in which thanks are being given to the gods for the victory of the Emperor Decius. He insults the sacrificing priests, and overturns and breaks the altars and statues. In what country in the world would such an outrage be overlooked? The Christian who in public tore down the edict of the Emperor Diocletian, and drew the great persecution upon his brethren in the last two years of the reign of that emperor, had more zeal than discretion, and, unhappily, brought a great disaster on the body

[1] I omit many of the lengthy notes, in which Voltaire, with veiled irony and a bland pretence of orthodoxy—for the reason of which see the Introduction—throws doubt on the persecutions. The freer scholarship of the nineteenth century has so far justified his scepticism that few are now interested in the fairy tales of the early " persecutions." There was only one general repression of the Christians, under Diocletian. See the latest editions of Gibbon, and Robertson's *Short History of Christianity* (pp. 130-140).—J. M.

to which he belonged. This unthinking zeal, which often broke out, and was condemned even by some of the fathers of the Church, was probably the cause of all the persecutions.

I do not, of course, compare the early Protestants with the early Christians; one cannot put error by the side of truth. But it is a fact that Forel, the predecessor of Calvin, did at Arles the same thing that St. Polyeuctes had done in Armenia. The statue of St. Antony the Hermit was being carried in procession, and Forel and some of his companions fell on the monks who carried it, beat and scattered them, and threw St. Antony in the river. He deserved the death which he managed to evade by flight.[1] If he had been content to call out to the monks that he did not believe that a crow brought half a loaf to St. Antony the Hermit, or that St. Antony conversed with centaurs and satyrs, he would merely have merited a stern rebuke for disturbing public order; and if, the evening after the procession, he had calmly studied the story of the crow, the centaurs, and the satyrs, they would have had no reproach to make him.

You think that the Romans would have suffered the infamous Antinous [2] to be raised to the rank of the secondary gods, and would have rent and given to the beasts those whose only reproach was to have quietly worshipped one just God! You imagine that they would have recognised a supreme and sovereign God, master of all the secondary gods, as we see in their formula, *Deus optimus maximus*, yet persecuted those who worshipped one sole God!

It is incredible that there was any inquisition against the Christians—that men were sent among them to interrogate them on their beliefs—under the emperors. On that point they never troubled either

---

[1] Voltaire's irony and pretence of orthodoxy must again, as in so many places, be taken into account. You do not, as a French commentator says, incur death in French law for throwing a piece of wood into the Rhone.—J. M.

[2] A beautiful youth loved by the Emperor Hadrian.—J. M.

Jew, Syrian, Egyptian, Druid, or philosopher. The martyrs were men who made an outcry against what they called false gods. It was a very wise and pious thing to refuse to believe·in them; but, after all, if, not content with worshipping God in spirit and in truth, they broke out violently against the established cult, however absurd it was, we are compelled to admit that they were themselves intolerant.[1]

Tertullian admits in his *Apology* (ch. xxxix.) that the Christians were regarded as seditious. The charge was unjust, but it shows that it was not merely their religion which stimulated the zeal of the magistrates. He admits that the Christians refused to decorate their doors with laurel branches in the public rejoicings for the victories of the emperors; such an affectation might easily be turned into the crime of treason.

The first period of juridical severity against the Christians was under Domitian, but it was generally restricted to a banishment that did not last a year. " Facile coeptum repressit, restitutis quos ipse relegaverat," says Tertullian [" He quickly repressed the work, restoring those whom he had banished "]. Lactantius, whose style is so vehement, agrees that the Church was peaceful and flourishing from Domitian to Decius [A.D. 96–250].[2] This long peace, he says, was broken when " that execrable animal Decius began to vex the Church."

[1] If they had been content to preach and write, they would probably have been left in peace; but the refusal to take the oaths, in a constitution in which much use was made of oaths, exposed them to suspicion. The refusal to take part publicly in the feasts in honour of the emperors was a sort of crime at a time when the empire was constantly stirred by revolutions. The insults they offered to the established cult were punished with severity and barbarism, and it was an age of rough and violent ways.

[2] *The Deaths of the Persecutors*, ch. iii.—a very untrustworthy work. It is doubtful if Lactantius wrote it. There was no general persecution under Domitian, but certain high officials suffered, like the rest of Rome, from his excessive suspicion.—J. M.

We need not discuss here the opinion of the learned Dodwell that the martyrs were few in number; but if the Romans persecuted the Christian religion, if the Senate had put to death so many innocent men with unusual tortures—plunging Christians in boiling oil and exposing girls naked to the beasts in the circus—how is it that they left untouched all the earlier bishops of Rome? St. Irenæus can count among them only one martyr, Telesphorus, in the year A.D. 139; and we have no proof that Telesphorus was put to death. Zepherinus governed the flock at Rome for twenty-eight years, and died peacefully in 219. It is true that nearly all the popes are inscribed in the early martyrologies, but the word "martyr" was then taken in its literal sense, as "witness," not as one put to death.

It is difficult to reconcile this persecuting fury with the freedom which the Christians had to hold the fifty-six Councils which ecclesiastical writers count in the first three centuries.

There were persecutions; but if they were as violent as we are told, it is probable that Tertullian, who wrote so vigorously against the established cult, would not have died in his bed. We know, of course, that the emperors would not read his *Apology*—an obscure work, composed in Africa, would hardly reach those who were ruling the world. But it must have been known to those who were in touch with the proconsul of Africa, and ought to have brought a good deal of ill-feeling on its author. He did not, however, suffer martyrdom.

Origen taught publicly at Alexandria, and was not put to death. This same Origen, who spoke so freely to both pagans and Christians—announcing Jesus to the former and denying a God in three persons to the latter—says expressly, in the third book of his *Contra Celsum*, that "there have been few martyrs, and those at long intervals"; although, he says, "the Christians do all in their power to make everybody embrace their religion, running about the towns and villages."

It is clear that a seditious complexion might be put by the hostile priests on all this running about, yet the missions were tolerated, in spite of the constant and cowardly disorders of the Egyptian people, who killed a Roman for slaying a cat, and were always contemptible.[1]

Who did more to bring upon him the priests and the government than St. Gregory Thaumaturgus, a pupil of Origen? Gregory saw, during the night, an old man, sent by God, and a woman shining with light; the woman was the Virgin, and the man St. John the Evangelist. John dictated to him a creed, which Gregory went out to preach. In going to Neocæsarea he passed by a temple in which oracles were given, and the rain compelled him to spend the night in it, after making many signs of the cross. The following day the sacrificing priest was astonished to find that the demons who were wont to answer him would do so no longer. When he called, they said that they would come no more, and could not live in the temple, because Gregory had spent the night in it and made the sign of the cross in it.

The priest had Gregory seized, and Gregory said : " I can expel the demons from wherever I like, and drive them into wherever I like." " Send them back into my temple, then," said the priest. So Gregory tore off a piece from a book he had in his hand and wrote on it : " Gregory to Satan : I order thee to return to this temple." The message was placed on the altar, and the demons obeyed, and gave the oracles as before.

St. Gregory of Nyssa tells us these facts in his *Life of St. Gregory Thaumaturgus*. The priests in charge of the idols must have been incensed against Gregory, and wished, in their blindness, to denounce him to the magistrates. But their greatest enemy never suffered persecution.

[1] Voltaire, who knew only the late history of Egypt, gives a lengthy note to explain his disdain. Archæological research has altered all that.—J. M.

It is said that St. Cyprian was the first bishop of
Carthage to be condemned to death, in the year 258.
During a very long period, therefore, no bishop of
Carthage suffered for his religion.   History does not
tell us what charges were made against St. Cyprian,
what enemies he had, and why the pro-consul of
Africa was angry with him.   St. Cyprian writes to
Cornelius, Bishop of Rome : " There was, a short time
ago, some popular disturbance at Carthage, and the
cry was twice raised that I ought to be cast to the
lions."   It is very probable that the excitement of
the passionate populace of Carthage was the cause
of the death of Cyprian ; it is, at all events, certain
that the Emperor Gallus did not condemn him on the
ground of religion from distant Rome, since he left
untouched Cornelius, who lived under his eyes.

So many hidden causes are associated at times with
the apparent cause, so many unknown springs may
be at work in the persecution of a man, that it is
impossible, centuries afterwards, to discover the
hidden source of the misfortunes even of distinguished
men ; it is still more difficult to explain the persecution of an individual who must have been known only
to those of his own party.

Observe that St. Gregory Thaumaturgus and St.
Denis, Bishop of Alexandria, who were not put to
death, lived at the same time as St. Cyprian.   How
is it that they were left in peace, since they were, at
least, as well known as the Bishop of Carthage?
And why was Cyprian put to death?   Does it not
seem as if the latter fell a victim to personal and
powerful enemies, under the pretext of calumny
or reasons of State, which are so often associated with
religion, and that the former were fortunate enough
to escape the malice of men ?

It is impossible that the mere charge of being a
Christian led to the death of St. Ignatius under the
clement and just Trajan, since the Christians were
allowed to accompany and console him during his
voyage to Rome.   Seditions were common at Antioch,

always a turbulent city, where Ignatius was secret bishop of the Christians. Possibly these seditions were imputed to the Christians, and brought the authorities upon them.

St. Simeon, for instance, was charged before Sapor with being a Roman spy. The story of his martyrdom tells that King Sapor ordered him to worship the sun, but we know that the Persians did not worship the sun; they regarded it as an emblem of the good principle Ormuzd, the god whom they recognised.

However tolerant we may be, we cannot help being indignant with the rhetoricians who accuse Diocletian of persecuting the Christians as soon as he ascended the throne. Let us consult Eusebius of Cæsarea, the favourite and panegyrist of Constantine, the violent enemy of preceding emperors. He says (*Ecclesiastical History*, Bk. VIII.): "The emperors for a long time gave the Christians proof of their goodwill. They entrusted provinces to them; several Christians lived in the palace; they even married Christians. Diocletian married Prisca, whose daughter was the wife of Maximianus Galerius."

We may well suspect that the persecution set afoot by Galerius, after a clement and benevolent reign of twenty-nine years, was due to some intrigue that is unknown to us.[1]

The story of the massacre of the Theban Legion on religious grounds is absurd. It is ridiculous to say that the legion came from Asia by the great St. Bernard Pass; it is impossible that it should be brought from Asia at all to quell a sedition in Gaul— a year after the sedition broke out, moreover; it is not less incredible that six thousand infantry and seven hundred cavalry could be slain in a pass in which

---

[1] Not wholly unknown. We know that the mother of Galerius, an ignorant peasant, was stung by the insults of Christian officers in the palace, and inflamed her son, who persuaded Diocletian to take action. The action was mild at first; but Christians tore down the imperial edict, and the palace was twice set on fire. Then Diocletian yielded.—J. M.

two hundred men could hold at bay a whole army. The account of this supposed butchery begins with an evident imposture : " When the earth groaned under the tyranny of Diocletian, heaven was peopled with saints." Now, this episode is supposed to have taken place in 286, a time when Diocletian favoured the Christians, and the empire flourished.[1] Finally— a point which might dispense us from discussion alto- gether—there never was a Theban Legion. The Romans had too much pride and common sense to make up a legion of Egyptians, who served only as slaves at Rome; one might as well talk of a Jewish Legion. We have the names of the thirty-two legions which represented the chief strength of the Roman Empire, and there is no Theban Legion among them. We must relegate the fable to the same category as the acrostic verses of the Sibyls, which foretold the miracles of Christ, and so many other forgeries with which a false zeal duped the credulous.

OF THE DANGER OF FALSE LEGENDS, AND OF PERSECUTION

Untruth has imposed on men too long; it is time to pick out the few truths that we can trace amid the clouds of legends which brood over Roman history after Tacitus and Suetonius, and have almost always enveloped the annals of other nations.

How can we believe, for instance, that the Romans, whose laws exhibit to us a people of grave and severe character, exposed to prostitution Christian virgins and young women of rank? It is a gross misunder- standing of the austere dignity of the makers of our laws, who punished so rigorously the frailties of their vestal virgins. The " Sincere Acts " of Ruinart describe these indignities; but are we to put the " Acts " of Ruinart on a level with the *Acts of the Apostles* ? These " Sincere Acts " say, according to

[1] The persecution under Diocletian began in 303.—J. M.

the Bollandists, that there were in the town of Ancyra seven Christian virgins, each about seventy years old; that the governor Theodectes condemned them to be handed over to the young men of the town; and that he changed the sentence, as was proper, and compelled them to assist, naked, in the mysteries of Diana—at which none ever assisted without a veil. St. Theodotus—who, to tell the truth, kept a public-house, but was not less zealous on that account—prayed ardently to God to take these holy maidens out of life, lest they should succumb to temptation. God heard him. The governor then had them thrown into a lake, with stones round their necks, and they at once appeared to Theodotus and begged him to see that their bodies were not eaten by fishes.

The holy publican and his companions went during the night to the shore of the lake, which was guarded by soldiers. A heavenly torch went before them, and when they came to the spot where the guards were, a heavenly cavalier, armed from top to toe, chased the guards, lance in hand. St. Theodotus drew from the lake the bodies of the virgins. He was brought before the governor—and the celestial cavalier did not prevent the soldiers from cutting off his head. We repeat that we venerate the real martyrs, but it is not easy to believe this story of the Bollandists and Ruinart.

Shall we tell the story of the young St. Romanus? He was cast into the flames, says Eusebius, and certain Jews who were present insulted Jesus Christ for allowing his followers to be burned, whereas God had withdrawn Shadrach, Meshach, and Abednego from the fiery furnace. Hardly had the Jews spoken when Romanus emerged in triumph from the flames. The emperor ordered that he should be pardoned, saying to the judge that he did not want to fall foul of God. Curious words for Diocletian! The judge, in spite of the emperor's pardon, ordered the tongue of Romanus to be cut out; and, although he had executioners, he had this operation performed by a physician. The young Romanus, who had stuttered from birth, spoke volubly as soon as his tongue was cut out. The physician, to show that the operation had been properly performed, took a man who was passing and cut off just as much of his tongue as he had done in the case of Romanus, and the man died. " Anatomy teaches us," says the author, learnedly, " that a man cannot live without a tongue." If Eusebius really wrote this nonsense, and the passage is not an interpolation, it is difficult to take his history seriously.

Then there is the martyrdom of St. Felicitas and her seven children, sent to death, it is said, by the wise and pious Antoninus. In this case it seems probable that some writer with more zeal than truthfulness has imitated the story of the Maccabees. The narrative begins : " St. Felicitas was a Roman, and lived in the reign of Antoninus." From these words it is clear that the author was not a contemporary of St. Felicitas. He says that the prætor sat to judge them in the Campus Martius. The forgery is exposed by this statement. The Campus Martius, which had once been used for the elections, then served for reviews of the troops and for military games. Again, it is said that after the trial the emperor entrusted the execution of the sentence to various judges; which is quite opposed to all procedure at that time or in our own.

Then there is a St. Hippolytus, who is supposed to have been dragged by horses, like Hippolytus the son of Theseus. This punishment was quite unknown to the Romans, and it is merely the similarity of name that has led to the invention of the legend.

You will observe in these accounts of the martyrs, which were composed entirely by the Christians themselves, that crowds of Christians always go freely to the prison of the condemned, follow him to the scaffold, receive his blood, bury his body, and work

miracles with his relics. If it were the religion alone
that was persecuted, would not the authorities have
arrested these declared Christians who assisted their
condemned brethren, and who were accused of per-
forming magic with the martyred bodies? Would
they not have been treated as we treated the Waldensians, the Albigenses, the Hussites, and the various
sects of Protestants? We slew them and burned them
in crowds, without distinction of age or sex. Is there,
in any reliable account of the ancient persecutions,
any single feature that approaches our massacre of
St. Bartholomew or the Irish massacres? Is there a
single one with any resemblance to the annual festival
that is still held at Toulouse—a cruel and damnable
festival, in which a whole people thanks God and
congratulates itself that it slew four thousand of its
fellow-citizens two hundred years ago?

I say it with a shudder, but it is true; it is we
Christians who have been the persecutors, the executioners, the assassins. And who were our victims?
Our brothers. It is we who have destroyed a hundred
towns, the crucifix or Bible in our hands, and have
incessantly shed blood and lit flames from the reign
of Constantine to the fury of the cannibals of the
Cévènes.

We still occasionally send to the gibbet a few poor
folk of Poitou, Vivarais, Valence, or Montauban.
Since 1745 [a period of seven years] we have hanged
eight of those men who are known as " preachers " or
" ministers of the gospel," whose only crime was
to have prayed God for the king in their native
dialect and given a drop of wine and a morsel of
leavened bread to a few silly peasants. These things
are not done at Paris, where pleasure is the only
thing of consequence, and people are ignorant of what
is done in the provinces and abroad. These trials are
over in an hour; they are shorter than the trial of a
deserter. If the king were aware of them, he would
put an end to them.

Catholic priests are not treated thus in any Pro-

testant country. There are more than a hundred
Catholic priests in England and Ireland; they are
known, and were untouched during the late war.

Shall we always be the last to embrace the wholesome ideas of other nations? They have amended
their ways; when shall we amend ours? It took us
sixty years to admit what Newton had demonstrated;
we are hardly beginning to save the lives of our
children by inoculation; and it is only recently that
we have begun to act on sound principles of agriculture. When shall we begin to act on sound
principles of humanity? How can we have the
audacity to reproach the pagans with making martyrs
when we have been guilty of the same cruelty in the
same circumstances?

Suppose we grant that the Romans put to death
numbers of Christians on purely religious grounds.
In that case the Romans were very much to blame.
Why should we be similarly unjust? Would we
become persecutors at the very time when we reproach
them with persecuting?

If any man were so wanting in good faith, or so
fanatical, as to say to me: " Why do you come to
expose our blunders and faults? Why do you
destroy our false miracles and false legends? They
nourish the piety of many people; there are such
things as necessary errors; do not tear out of the
body an incurable ulcer if it would entail the destruction of the body." I should reply to this man: All
these false miracles by which you shake the trust that
should be given to real ones, all these absurd legends
which you add to the truths of the gospels, extinguish
religion in the hearts of men. Too many people who
long for instruction, and have not the time to instruct
themselves, say: " The heads of my religion have
deceived me, therefore there is no religion. It is
better to cast oneself into the arms of nature than into
those of error; I would rather depend on the law of
nature than on the inventions of men." Some are so
unfortunate as to go even farther. They see that

imposture put a curb on them, and they will not have even the curb of truth. They lean to atheism. They become depraved, because others have been false and cruel.

These, assuredly, are the consequences of all the pious frauds and all the superstitions. The reasoning of men is, as a rule, only half-reasoning. It is a very poor argument to say : " Voraginé, the author of the *Golden Legend*, and the Jesuit Ribadeneira, compiler of the *Flowers of the Saints*, wrote sheer nonsense; therefore there is no God. The Catholics have murdered a certain number of Huguenots, and the Huguenots have murdered a certain number of Catholics; therefore there is no God. Men have made use of confession, communion, and all the other sacraments, to commit the most horrible crimes; therefore there is no God." I should conclude, on the contrary : Therefore there is a God who, after this transitory life, in which we have known him so little, and committed so many crimes in his name, will vouchsafe to console us for our misfortunes. For, considering the wars of religion, the forty papal schisms (nearly all of which were bloody), the impostures which have nearly all been pernicious, the irreconcilable hatreds lit by differences of opinion, and all the evils that false zeal has brought upon them, men have long suffered hell in this world.

ABUSES OF INTOLERANCE

Do I propose, then, that every citizen shall be free to follow his own reason, and believe whatever this enlightened or deluded reason shall dictate to him? Certainly, provided he does not disturb the public order. It does not depend on man to believe or not to believe; but it depends on him to respect the usages of his country. If you insist that it is a crime to disbelieve in the dominant religion, you condemn the first Christians, your fathers, and you justify those whom you reproach with persecuting them.

You say that there is a great difference; that all other religions are the work of man, and the Catholic, Apostolic, and Roman Church alone is the work of God. But, surely, the fact that our religion is divine does not imply that it should rule by hatred, fury, exile, the confiscation of goods, imprisonment, torture, murder, and thanksgiving to God for murder? The more divine the Christian religion is, the less it is the place of man to command it; if God is its author, he will maintain it without your aid. You know well that intolerance begets only hypocrites or rebels. Fearful alternative! Would you, indeed, sustain by executioners the religion of a God who fell into the hands of executioners, and who preached only gentleness and patience?

Reflect on the frightful consequences of the right of intolerance. If it were allowed to despoil, cast in prison, and put to death a citizen, who at a certain degree of latitude, would not profess the religion generally admitted at that degree, how could we except the leaders of the State from those penalties? Religion equally binds the monarch and the beggar; hence more than fifty doctors or monks have made the monstrous assertion that it was lawful to depose or slay any sovereign who dissented from the dominant religion, and the Parliaments of our kingdom have repeatedly condemned these abominable decisions of abominable theologians.[1]

---

[1] The Jesuit Busenbaum, edited by the Jesuit La Croix, says that " it is lawful to kill a prince excommunicated by the Pope, in whatever country he may be found, because the universe belongs to the Pope, and he who accepts this commission does a charitable deed." This proposition, drawn up in the antechambers of hell, has done more than anything to raise France against the Jesuits. [They were expelled from France in 1767.—J. M.]. They endeavoured to justify themselves by pointing out that the same conclusions are found in St. Thomas and other Dominicans. As a matter of fact, St. Thomas of Aquin, the " angelic doctor " and " interpreter of the divine will "—such are his titles—says that an apostate prince loses his right to the crown, and should no longer be obeyed (Bk. II., Part II., quest. xii.); that the

The blood of Henry the Great [IV.] was still warm when the Parlement de Paris issued a decree making the independence of the Crown a fundamental law. Cardinal Duperron, who owed his position to Henry the Great, arose in the States of 1614 against the decree of the Parlement, and had it suppressed. All the journals of the time record the terms which Duperron used in his discourse : " If a prince became an Arian," he said, " we should be obliged to depose him."

Let us be allowed to say that every citizen is entitled to inherit his father's property, and that we do not see why he should be deprived of it, and dragged to the gibbet, because he takes sides with one theologian against another.

We know that our dogmas were not always clearly explained and universally received in the Church. Christ not having said in what manner the Holy Ghost proceeded, the Latin Church long believed with the Greek that he proceeded from the Father only; after a time it added, in the Creed, that he also proceeded from the Son. I ask whether, the day after this decision, any citizen who preferred to keep to the old formula deserved to be put to death ? But is it less unjust and cruel to punish to-day the man who thinks as people thought in former times ? Were men guilty in the days of Honorius I. because they did not believe that Jesus had two wills ?

It is not long since the Immaculate Conception began to be generally accepted; the Dominicans still refuse to believe it.[1] At what particular date will these Dominicans incur the penalties of heresy in this world and the next ?

Church may punish him with death; that the Emperor Julian was tolerated only because the Christians were weak (same passage); that it is right to kill any heretic (same place, questions xi. and xii.); that those are laudable who free a people from a tyrannical prince, etc. We must admit that Gerson, Chancellor of the University, went farther than St. Thomas, and the Franciscan Jean Petit much farther than Gerson.

[1] It was not defined by the Church until 1854.—J. M.

If we need a lesson how to behave in these interminable disputes, we should look to the apostles and evangelists. There was ground for a violent schism between Peter and Paul, and Paul withstood Peter to the face, but the controversy was peacefully settled. The evangelists in turn had a great field of combat, if they had resembled modern writers. They contradict each other frequently; yet we find no dissension among their followers over these contradictions, and they are neatly reconciled by the fathers of the Church. St. Paul, in his epistle to a few Jews at Rome who had been converted to Christianity, says at the end of the third chapter that faith alone glorifies, and works justify no one. St. James, on the contrary, in his epistle (ch. ii.) says constantly that one cannot be saved without works. Here is a point that has separated two great sects among us, yet made no division among the apostles.

If the persecution of those with whom we dispute were a holy action, the man who had killed most heretics would be the greatest saint in Paradise. What a poor figure the man who had been content to despoil and imprison his brothers would cut by the side of the zealot who had slain hundreds of them on St. Bartholomew's day! Here is a proof of it. The successor of St. Peter and his consistory cannot err. They approved, acclaimed, and consecrated the massacre of St. Bartholomew. Therefore this deed was holy; and therefore of two assassins who were equal in piety one who had killed twenty-four Huguenot women would have double the glory of the man who had killed only a dozen. By the same reasoning the fanatics of Cévènes would have ground to believe that they would be elevated in glory in proportion to the number of priests, monks, and Catholic women they had slain. It is a strange title to glory in heaven.

WHETHER INTOLERANCE WAS OF DIVINE RIGHT IN JUDAISM, AND WHETHER IT WAS ALWAYS PRACTISED [1]

Divine right means, I believe, the precepts which God himself has given. He ordered that the Jews should eat a lamb cooked with lettuces, and that the eaters should stand, with a stick in their hands, in commemoration of the Passover; he commanded that in the consecration of the high-priest blood should be applied to his right ear, right hand, and right foot. They seem curious customs to us, but they were not to antiquity. He ordered them to put the iniquities of the people on the goat *hazazel*, and forbade them to eat scaleless fishes, hares, hedgehogs, owls, griffins, etc. He instituted feasts and ceremonies.

All these things, which seem arbitrary to other nations, and a matter of positive law and usage, being ordered by God himself, became a divine law to the Jews, just as whatever Christ ordered is a divine law for us. Let us not inquire why God substituted a new law for that which he gave to Moses, and why he laid more commandments on Moses than on Abraham, and more on Abraham than on Noah. It seems that he deigns to accommodate himself to the times and the state of the human race. It is a kind of paternal gradation. But these abysses are too deep for our feeble sight. Let us keep to our subject, and see first what intolerance was among the Jews.

It is true that in *Exodus, Numbers, Leviticus*, and *Deuteronomy* there are very severe laws, and even more severe punishments, in connection with religion. Many commentators find a difficulty in reconciling the words of Moses with the words of Jeremiah and Amos, and those of the celebrated speech of St.

[1] This section is somewhat abridged, as much of it is better developed in preceding works.—J. M.

Stephen in *Acts*. Amos says that in the deserts the
Jews worshipped Moloch, Rempham, and Kium.
Jeremiah says explicitly (vii. 12) that God asked no
sacrifice of their fathers when they came out of
Egypt. St. Stephen says in his speech to the Jews
(*Acts* vii. 42) : " Then God turned and gave them up
to worship the host of heaven ; as it is written in the
book of the prophets, O ye house of Israel, have ye
offered to me slain beasts and sacrifices for the space
of forty years in the wilderness ? Yea, ye took up
the tabernacle of Moloch, and the star of your god
Rempham."

Other critics infer that these gods were tolerated by
Moses, and they quote these words of *Deuteronomy*
(xii. 8) : " When ye are in the land of Canaan, ye
shall not do all the things that we do here this day,
where every man does what he pleases." They find
encouragement in the fact that nothing is said of
any religious act of the people in the desert, and there
is no mention of Passover, Pentecost, Feast of Taber-
nacles, or public prayer in any shape. Circumcision,
moreover, the seal of the covenant, was not practised.

It is enough, it seems to me, that it is proved by
Holy Scripture that, in spite of the extraordinary
punishment inflicted on the Jews on account of the
cult of Apis, they had complete liberty for a long time.
Possibly the massacre of twenty-three thousand men
by Moses for worshipping the golden calf set up by his
brother led him to appreciate that nothing was gained
by severity, and induced him to close his eyes to the
people's passion for strange gods.

Sometimes he seems to transgress his own law. He
forbade the making of images, yet set up a brazen
serpent. We find another deviation from the law
in the temple of Solomon. He had twelve oxen carved
to sustain the great basin of the temple, and in the
ark were placed cherubim with the heads of eagles
and calves. It seems to have been this calf-head,
badly made, and found in the temple by Roman

soldiers, which led to the belief that the Jews worshipped an ass.

The worship of foreign gods was vainly prohibited.
Solomon was quite at his ease in idolatry. Jeroboam,
to whom God had given ten parts of the kingdom,
set up two golden calves, and ruled for twenty-two
years, uniting in his person the dignities of monarch
and pontiff. The little kingdom of Judah under
Rehoboam raised altars and statues to foreign gods.
The holy king Asa did not destroy the high places.
The high-priest Urijah erects in the temple, in the
place of the altar of holocausts, an altar to the king
of Syria (2 *Kings* xvi.). In a word, there seems to be
no real restraint in matters of religion. I know that
the majority of the Jewish kings murdered each other,
but that was always to further a material interest, not
on account of belief.[1]

It is true that some of the prophets secured the
interest of heaven in their vengeance. Elias brought
down fire from heaven to consume the priests of Baal.
Elisha caused forty-two bears to devour the children
who commented on his baldness. But these are rare
miracles, and facts that it would be rather hard to
wish to imitate.

It is also objected that the Jewish people were very
ignorant and barbaric. In the war with the Midianites Moses ordered that all the male children and their
mothers should be slain and the booty divided.
Some commentators even argue that thirty-two girls
were sacrificed to the Lord : " The Lord's tribute
was thirty and two persons [virgins] " (*Numbers*
xxxii. 40). That the Jews did offer human sacrifices
is seen in the story of Jephthah [*Judges* xi. 39], and
the cutting-up of king Agag by the priest Samuel.

[1] Voltaire's eagerness to show the tolerance of the Jews
is purely paradoxical and ironical. His sole object in this
section is to expose the crudities of the Old Testament,
under the cloak of orthodox theological reasoning. Hence
he omits the savage laws of Deuteronomy against foreign
cults.—J. M.

Ezekiel even promises that they will eat human flesh : " Ye shall eat the horse and the rider; ye shall drink the blood of princes." Some commentators apply two verses of this prophecy to the Jews themselves, and the others to the carnivorous beasts. We do not find in the whole history of this people any mark of generosity, magnanimity, or beneficence; yet some ray of toleration escapes always from the cloud of their long and frightful barbarism.

The story of Micah and the Levite, told in chapters xvii. and xviii. of *Judges*, is another incontestable proof of the great liberty and toleration that prevailed among the Jews. Micah's wife, a rich Ephraimite woman, had lost eleven hundred pieces of silver. Her son restored them to her, and she devoted them to the Lord, making images of him, and built a small chapel. A Levite served the chapel, receiving ten pieces of silver, a tunic, and a cloak every year, besides his food; and Micah said : " Now know I the Lord will do me good, seeing I have a Levite to my priest " (xvii. 13).

However, six hundred men of the tribe of Dan, who wanted to seize some village of the district to settle in, and had no priest-Levite to secure the favour of God for their enterprise, went to Micah's house, and took the ephod, idols, and Levite, in spite of the remonstrances of the priest and the cries of Micah and his mother. They then proceeded with confidence to attack the village of Lais, and put everything in it to fire and sword, as was their custom. They gave the name of Dan to Lais in honour of their victory, and set Micah's idol on an altar; and, what is still more remarkable, Jonathan, grandson of Moses, was the high priest of this temple, in which the God of Israel and Micah's idol were worshipped.

After the death of Gideon the Hebrews worshipped Baal-berith for nearly twenty years, and gave up the cult of Adonai; and no leader or judge or priest cried for vengeance. Their crime was great, I admit; but if such idolatry was tolerated, how much the more easily should we tolerate differences within the proper cult.

Some allege as a proof of intolerance that, when the Lord himself had allowed his ark to be taken by the Philistines in a battle, the only punishment he inflicted on the Philistines was a secret disease, resembling hemorrhoids, the overthrowing of the statue of Dagon, and the sending of a number of rats into their country. And when the Philistines, to appease his anger, had sent back the ark, drawn by two cows, which had calves, and offered to God five golden rats and five golden anuses, the Lord slew seventy elders of Israel and fifty thousand of the people for looking at the ark. The answer is plain, therefore: the Lord's chastisement is not connected with belief, or difference of cult, or idolatry.

Had the Lord wished to punish idolatry, he would have slain all the Philistines who dared to take his ark, and who worshipped Dagon; but he slew instead fifty thousand and seventy men of his own people merely because they looked at an ark at which they ought not to have looked. So different are the laws, the morals, and the economy of the Jews from anything that we know to-day; so far are the inscrutable ways of God above our own! However, God is not punishing a foreign cult, but a profanation of his own, an indiscreet curiosity, an act of disobedience, possibly a spirit of revolt. We realise that such chastisements belong to God only in the Jewish theocracy. We cannot repeat too often that these times and ways have no relation to our own.

Again, when in later years the idolatrous Naaman asked Elisha if he were allowed to accompany his king to the temple of Rimmon, and worship with him, Elisha—the man who caused children to be devoured by bears—merely said, "Go in peace." More remarkable still is the fact that the Lord orders Jeremiah to put cords and yokes round his neck, and send them to the kings of Moab, Ammon, Edom, Tyre, and Sidon, saying, on the part of the Lord: "I have given all your lands to Nebuchadnezzar, king of Babylon, my servant." Here we have an idolatrous king declared to be the servant and favourite of God.

The same Jeremiah, whom the petty king of the Jews, Zedekiah, had put in prison and then pardoned, advises the king, on the part of God, to surrender to the king of Babylon. Thus God takes the part of an idolatrous king. He gives him possession of the ark, the mere sight of which had cost fifty thousand and seventy Jews their lives, the holy of holies, and the rest of the temple, the building of which had cost a hundred and eight thousand gold talents, a million and seventeen thousand silver talents, and ten thousand gold drachmas, left by David and his officers for the construction of the house of the Lord; which, without counting the funds used by Solomon, amounts to nineteen thousand and sixty-two million francs, or thereabouts, of our money [more than £750,000,000]. Never was idolatry so signally rewarded! I am aware that the figure is exaggerated, and may be due to a copyist; but if you reduce the sum by half, or to a fourth or an eighth, it is still astonishing. One is hardly less surprised at the wealth which Herodotus says he saw in the temple of Ephesus. But treasures are nothing in the eyes of God; the title of his " servant," which is given to Nebuchadnezzar, is the only real treasure.

God is equally favourable to Kir, or Koresh, or Kosroes, whom we call Cyrus. He calls him " his Christ," " his Anointed," although he was not anointed in the ordinary meaning of the word, and he followed the religion of Zoroaster; he calls him his " shepherd," though he was a usurper in the eyes of men. There is no greater mark of predilection in the whole of Scripture.

You read in *Malachi* that " from the east to the west the name of God is great among the nations, and pure oblations are everywhere offered to him." God takes as much care of the idolatrous Ninevites as of the Jews; he threatens and pardons them. Mel-

chizedech, who was not a Jew, sacrificed to God.   The
idolatrous Balaam was a prophet.   Scripture shows,
therefore, that God not only tolerated other peoples,
but took a paternal care of them.   And we dare to
be intolerant !

EXTREME TOLERANCE OF THE JEWS

Hence both under Moses, the judges, and the kings
you find constant instances of toleration.   Moses
says several times (*Exodus* xx.) that " God punishes
the fathers in the children, down to the fourth generation "; and it was necessary thus to threaten a people
to whom God had not revealed the immortality of
the soul, or the punishments and rewards of another
life.   These truths were not made known either in
the Decalogue or any part of *Leviticus* or *Deuteronomy*.
They were dogmas of the Persians, Babylonians,
Egyptians, Greeks, and Cretans; but they by no
means formed part of the Jewish religion.   Moses
does not say : " Honour thy father and thy mother
if thou wouldst go to heaven "; but : " Honour thy
father and thy mother, that thou mayst live long on
the earth."   He threatens the Jews only with bodily
maladies and other material evils.   Nowhere does he
tell them that their immortal souls will be tortured
after death or be rewarded.   God, who himself led
his people, punished or rewarded them at once for
their good or bad actions.   Everything was temporal.
Those who ignorantly maintain that Moses taught the
immortality of the soul strip the New Testament of
one of its greatest advantages over the Old Testament.
It is certain that the law of Moses spoke only of
temporal chastisement, down to the fourth generation.
However, in spite of the precise formulation of this
law and the express declaration of God that he would
punish down to the fourth generation, Ezekiel
announces the very opposite to the Jews.   He says
(xviii. 20) that the son will not bear the iniquity of his
father; and he even goes so far as to make God say

that he had given them " statutes that were not good " (xx. 25).

The book of Ezekiel was nevertheless inserted in the canon of inspired writers. It is true that the synagogue did not allow anyone to read it until he was thirty years old, as St. Jerome tells us; but that was in order that young men might not make evil use of the too candid pictures of vice in chapters xvi. and xxiii. The book was always received, in spite of the fact that it expressly contradicted Moses.

When the immortality of the soul was at length admitted, which probably began about the time of the Babylonian captivity, the Sadducees continued to believe that there were no punishments and rewards after death, and that the power of feeling and thinking perished with us, like the power of walking and digesting. They denied the existence of angels. They differed from the other Jews much more than Protestants differ from Catholics, yet they remained in the communion of their brethren. Some of their sect even became high-priests.

The Pharisees believed in fatalism and metempsychosis. The Essenians thought that the souls of the just went to the Fortunate Islands, and those of the wicked into a kind of Tartarus. They offered no sacrifices, and met in a special synagogue. Thus, when we look closely into Judaism, we are astonished to find the greatest toleration in the midst of the most barbaric horrors. It is a contradiction, we must admit; nearly all nations have been ruled by contradictions. Happy the contradiction that brings gentler ways into a people with bloody laws.

WHETHER INTOLERANCE WAS TAUGHT BY CHRIST

Let us now see whether Jesus Christ set up sanguinary laws, enjoined intolerance, ordered the building of dungeons of the inquisition, or instituted bodies of executioners.

There are, if I am not mistaken, few passages in the gospels from which the persecuting spirit might deduce that intolerance and constraint are lawful. One is the parable in which the kingdom of heaven is compared to a king who invites his friends to the wedding-feast of his son (*Matthew* xxii.). The king says to them, by means of his servants : " My oxen and my fatlings are killed, and all things are ready. Come unto the marriage." Some go off to their country houses, without taking any notice of the invitation; others go about their business; others assault and slay the king's servants. The king sends his army against the murderers, and destroys their town. He then sends out on the high road to bring in to the feast all who can be found. One of these sits at table without a wedding dress, and is put in irons and cast into outer darkness.

It is clear that, as this allegory concerns only the kingdom of heaven, it certainly does not give a man the right to strangle or put in jail a neighbour who comes to sup with him not wearing a festive garment. I do not remember reading anywhere in history of a prince who had a courtier arrested on that ground. It is hardly more probable that, if an emperor sent his pages to tell the princes of his empire that he had killed his fatlings and invited them to supper, the princes would kill the pages. The invitation to the feast means selection for salvation; the murder of the king's envoys represents the persecution of those who preach wisdom and virtue.

The other parable (*Luke* xiv.) tells of a man who invites his friends to a grand supper. When he is ready to sit at table, he sends his servant to inform them. One pleads that he has bought an estate, and must go to visit it; as one does not usually go to see an estate during the night, the excuse does not hold. Another says that he has bought five pairs of oxen, and must try them; his excuse is as weak as the preceding—one does not try oxen during the night. A third replies that he has just married; and that,

assuredly, is a good excuse. Then the holder of the
banquet angrily summons the blind and the lame to
the feast, and, seeing that there are still empty places,
says to his valet : " Go out into the highways and
hedges, and compel them to come in."

It is true that this parable is not expressly said to
be a figure of the kingdom of heaven. There has, unhappily, been too much abuse of these words, " Compel them to come in " ; but it is obvious that a single
valet could not forcibly compel all the people he meets
to come and sup with his master. Moreover, com-
pulsory guests of this sort would not make the dinner
very agreeable. According to the weightiest commentators, " Compel them to come in " merely means
" Beg, entreat, and press them to come in." What, I
ask you, have this entreaty and supper to do with
persecution?

If you want to take things literally, will you say
that a man must be blind and lame, and compelled by
force, to be in the bosom of the Church? Jesus says
in the same parable : " When thou makest a dinner or
supper, call not thy friends, nor thy brethren, neither
thy kinsmen, nor thy rich neighbours." Has anyone
ever inferred from this that we must not dine with
our kinsmen and friends when they have acquired a
little money?

After the parable of the feast Christ says (*Luke* xiv.
26) : " If any man come to me, and hate not his father,
and mother, and wife, and children, and brethren,
and sisters, yea, and his own life also, he cannot be
my disciple. . . . For which of you, intending to
build a tower, sitteth not down first and counteth
the cost? " Is there anybody in the world so unnatural as to conclude that one must hate one's
father and mother? Is it not clear that the meaning
is : Do not hesitate between me and your dearest
affections?

The passage in *Matthew* (xviii. 17) is quoted : " If
he neglect to hear the Church, let him be unto thee
as an heathen man and a publican." That does not

absolutely say we must persecute pagans and the farmers of the king's taxes; they are cursed, it is true, but they are not handed over to the secular arm. Instead of the prerogatives of citizenship being taken from these farmers of taxes, they have received the greatest privileges. It is the only profession that is condemned in Scripture, and the one most in favour with governments. Why, then, should we not be as indulgent to our erring brethren as to the tax-gatherers?

The persecuting spirit further seeks a justification of itself in the driving of the merchants from the temple and the sending of a legion of demons from the body of a possessed man into the bodies of two thousand unclean animals. But who can fail to see that these are instances of the justice which God deigns to render to himself for the contravention of his law? It was a lack of respect for the house of the Lord to change its purview into a merchant's shop. It is no use saying that the Sanhedrim and the priests permitted this only for the sake of the sacrifices. The God to whom the sacrifices were made might assuredly destroy this profanation, though he was hidden in a human form; he might also punish those who introduced into the country such enormous herds of animals forbidden by a law which he deigned to observe himself. These cases have no relation whatever to persecution on account of dogma. The spirit of intolerance must be very poor in argument to appeal to such foolish pretexts.

Nearly all the rest of the words and actions of Christ breathe gentleness, patience, and indulgence. He does not even break out against Judas, who must betray him; he commands Peter never to use the sword; he reproaches the children of Zebedee, who, after the example of Elias, wanted to bring fire from heaven on a town that refused them shelter.

In the end Christ succumbed to the wicked. If one may venture to compare the sacred with the profane—God with a man—his death, humanly speaking, had some resemblance to the death of Socrates. The Greek philosopher was a victim to the hatred of the sophists, priests, and leaders of the people; the legislator of the Christians was destroyed by the Scribes, Pharisees, and priests. Socrates might have escaped death, and would not; Jesus Christ offered himself voluntarily. The Greek philosopher not only pardoned his calumniators and his wicked judges, but begged them to treat his children in the same way if they should ever be so fortunate as, like himself, to incur their hatred; the legislator of the Christians, infinitely superior, begged his father to forgive his enemies.

If it be objected that, while Socrates was calm, Jesus Christ seemed to fear death, and suffered such extreme anguish that he sweated blood—the strongest and rarest symptom of fear—this was because he deigned to stoop to all the weakness of the human body that he had put on. His body trembled—his soul was invincible. He taught us that true strength and grandeur consist in supporting the evils under which our nature succumbs. It is a splendid act of courage to meet death while you fear it.

Socrates had treated the sophists as ignorant men, and convinced them of bad faith; Jesus, using his divine rights, treated the Scribes and Pharisees as hypocrites, fools, blind and wicked men, serpents, and vipers.

Need I now ask whether it is tolerance or intolerance that is of divine right? If you wish to follow Jesus Christ, be martyrs, not executioners.

THE ONLY CASES IN WHICH INTOLERANCE IS HUMANLY LAWFUL

For a government to have the right to punish the errors of men it is necessary that their errors must take the form of crime; they do not take the form of crime unless they disturb society; they disturb society when they engender fanaticism;

hence men must avoid fanaticism in order to deserve toleration.

If a few young Jesuits, knowing that the Church has condemned the Jansenists, proceed to burn a house of the Oratorian priests because the Oratorian Quesnel was a Jansenist, it is clear that these Jesuits ought to be punished.

Again, if the Jesuits have acted upon improper maxims, and their institute is contrary to the laws of the kingdom, their society must be dissolved, and the Jesuits must be abolished and turned into citizens. The evil done to them is imaginary—the good is real. What hardship is there in wearing a short coat instead of a long black robe, and being free instead of being a slave?

If the Franciscan monks, carried away by a holy zeal for the Virgin Mary, go and destroy a Dominican convent, because the Dominicans believe that Mary was born in original sin, it will be necessary to treat the Franciscans in much the same way as the Jesuits.

We may say the same of the Lutherans and Calvinists. It is useless for them to say that they follow the promptings of their consciences, that it is better to obey God than men, or that they are the true flock, and must exterminate the wolves. In such cases they are wolves themselves.

One of the most remarkable examples of fanaticism is found in a small Danish sect, whose principle was excellent. They desired to secure eternal salvation for their brethren; but the consequences of the principle were peculiar. They knew that all infants which die unbaptised are damned, and that those which are so fortunate as to die immediately after baptism enjoy eternal glory. They therefore proceeded to kill all the newly-baptised boys and girls that they could find. No doubt this was a way of securing for them the highest conceivable happiness and preserving them from the sin and misery of this life. But these charitable folk forgot that it is not lawful to do a little evil that a great good may follow; that they had no right to the lives of these children; that the majority of parents are carnal enough to prefer to keep their children rather than see them slain in order to enter paradise; and that the magistrate has to punish homicide, even when it is done with a good intention.

The Jews would seem to have a better right than any to rob and kill us. Though there are a hundred instances of toleration in the Old Testament, there are also some instances and laws of severity. God has at times commanded them to kill idolaters, and reserve only the marriageable girls. Now they regard us as idolaters, and, although we tolerate them to-day, it is possible that, if they became masters, they would suffer only our girls to live.

They would, at least, be absolutely compelled to slay all the Turks, because the Turks occupy the lands of the Hittites, Jerbusites, Amorrhæans, Jersensæans, Hevæans, Aracæans, Cinæans, Hamatæans, and Samaritans. All these peoples were anathematised, and their country, which was more than seventy-five miles long, was given to the Jews in several consecutive covenants. They ought to regain their possessions, which the Mohammedans have usurped for the last thousand years.

If the Jews were now to reason in this way, it is clear that the only reply we should make would be to put them in the galleys.

These are almost the only cases in which intolerance seems reasonable.

ACCOUNT OF A CONTROVERSIAL DISPUTE IN CHINA

In the early years of the reign of the great Emperor Kam-hi a mandarin of the city of Canton heard from his house a great noise, which proceeded from the next house. He inquired if anybody was being killed, and was told that the almoner of the Danish missionary society, a chaplain from Batavia, and a Jesuit were disputing. He had them brought to his house, put tea and sweets before them, and asked why they quarrelled.

The Jesuit replied that it was very painful for him, since he was always right, to have to do with men who were always wrong; that he had at first argued with the greatest restraint, but had at length lost patience.

The mandarin, with the utmost discretion, reminded them that politeness was needed in all discussion, told them that in China men never became angry, and asked the cause of the dispute.

The Jesuit answered : " My lord, I leave it to you to decide. These two gentlemen refuse to submit to the decrees of the Council of Trent."

" I am astonished," said the mandarin. Then, turning to the refractory pair, he said : " Gentlemen, you ought to respect the opinions of a large gathering. I do not know what the Council of Trent is, but a number of men are always better informed than a single one. No one ought to imagine that he is better than others, and has a monopoly of reason. So our great Confucius teaches; and, believe me, you will do well to submit to the Council of Trent."

The Dane then spoke. " My lord speaks with the greatest wisdom," he said; " we respect great councils, as is proper, and therefore we are in entire agreement with several that were held before the Council of Trent."

" Oh, if that is the case," said the mandarin, " I beg your pardon. You may be right. So you and this Dutchman are of the same opinion, against this poor Jesuit."

" Not a bit," said the Dutchman. " This fellow's opinions are almost as extravagant as those of the Jesuit yonder, who has been so very amiable to you. I can't bear them."

" I don't understand," said the mandarin. " Are you not all three Christians? Have you not all three come to teach Christianity in our empire? Ought you not, therefore, to hold the same dogmas? "

" It is this way, my lord," said the Jesuit; " these

two are mortal enemies, and are both against me. Hence it is clear that they are both wrong, and I am right."

"That is not quite clear," said the mandarin; "strictly speaking, all three of you may be wrong. I should like to hear you all, one after the other."

The Jesuit then made a rather long speech, during which the Dane and the Dutchman shrugged their shoulders. The mandarin did not understand a word of it. Then the Dane spoke; the two opponents regarded each other with pity, and the mandarin again failed to understand. The Dutchman had the same effect. In the end they all spoke together and abused each other roundly. The good mandarin secured silence with great difficulty, and said : "If you want us to tolerate your teaching here, begin by being yourselves neither intolerant nor intolerable."

When they went out the Jesuit met a Dominican friar, and told him that he had won, adding that truth always triumphed. The Dominican said : "Had I been there, you would not have won; I should have convicted you of lying and idolatry." The quarrel became warm, and the Jesuit and Dominican took to pulling each other's hair. The mandarin, on hearing of the scandal, sent them both to prison. A sub-mandarin said to the judge : "How long does your excellency wish them to be kept in prison?" "Until they agree," said the judge. "Then," said the sub-mandarin, "they are in prison for life." "In that case," said the judge, "until they forgive each other." "They will never forgive each other," said the other; "I know them." "Then," said the mandarin, "let them stop there until they pretend to forgive each other."

WHETHER IT IS USEFUL TO MAINTAIN THE PEOPLE IN SUPERSTITION

Such is the weakness, such the perversity, of the human race that it is better, no doubt, for it to be

subject to all conceivable superstitions, provided
they be not murderous, than to live without religion.
Man has always needed a curb; and, although it
was ridiculous to sacrifice to fauns or naiads, it was
much more reasonable and useful to worship these
fantastic images of the deity than to sink into atheism.
A violent atheist would be as great a plague as a
violent superstitious man.

When men have not sound ideas of the divinity,
false ideas will take their place; just as, in ages of
impoverishment, when there is not sound money,
people use bad coin. The pagan feared to commit
a crime lest he should be punished by his false gods;
the Asiatic fears the chastisement of his pagoda.
Religion is necessary wherever there is a settled society.
The laws take care of known crimes; religion watches
secret crime.

But once men have come to embrace a pure and
holy religion, superstition becomes, not merely
useless, but dangerous. We must not feed on acorns
those to whom God offers bread.

Superstition is to religion what astrology is to
astronomy—the mad daughter of a wise mother.
These daughters have too long dominated the earth.

When, in our ages of barbarism, there were scarcely
two feudal lords who had a New Testament in their
homes, it might be pardonable to press fables on the
vulgar; that is to say, on these feudal lords, their weak-
minded wives, and their brutal vassals. They were
led to believe that St. Christopher had carried the
infant Jesus across a river; they were fed with stories
of sorcery and diabolical possession; they readily
believed that St. Genou healed gout, and St. Claire
sore eyes. The children believed in the werewolf,
and their parents in the girdle of St. Francis. The
number of relics was incalculable.

The sediment of these superstitions remained among
the people even when religion had been purified. We
know that when M. de Noailles, Bishop of Chalons,
removed and threw in the fire the pretended relic of

the sacred navel of Jesus Christ the town of Chalons took proceedings against him. But his courage was equal to his piety, and he succeeded in convincing the people that they could worship Jesus Christ in spirit and truth without having his navel in their church.

The Jansenists contributed not a little gradually to root out from the mind of the nation the false ideas that dishonoured the Christian religion. People ceased to believe that it sufficed to pray for thirty days to the Virgin to obtain all that they wished, and sin with impunity.

In the end the citizens began to suspect that it was not really St. Genevieve who gave or withheld rain, but God himself who disposed of the elements. The monks were astonished to see that their saints no longer worked miracles. If the writers of the life of St. Francis Xavier returned to this world, they would not dare to say that the saint raised nine people from the dead, that he was in two places at the same time, and that, when his crucifix fell into the sea, a crab restored it to him.

It is the same with excommunication. Historians tell us that when King Robert had been excommunicated by Pope Gregory V., for marrying his godmother, the Princess Bertha, his servants threw out of the window the meat served up to the king, and Queen Bertha was delivered of a goose, in punishment of the incestuous marriage. I doubt if in our time the waiters of the king of France would, if he were excommunicated, throw his dinner out of the window, and whether the queen would give birth to a gosling.

There remain, it is true, a few bigoted fanatics in the suburbs; but the disease, like vermin, attacks only the lowest of the populace. Every day reason penetrates farther into France, into the shops of merchants as well as the mansions of lords. We must cultivate the fruits of reason, the more willingly since it is now impossible to prevent them from developing. France, enlightened by Pascal, Nicole,

Arnaud, Bossuet, Descartes, Gassendi, Bayle, Fontenelle, etc., cannot be ruled as it was ruled in earlier times.

If the masters of error—the grand masters—so long paid and honoured for brutalising the human species, ordered us to-day to believe that the seed must die in order to germinate; that the earth stands motionless on its foundations—that it does not travel round the sun; that the tides are not a natural effect of gravitation; that the rainbow is not due to the refraction and reflection of light, etc., and based their decrees on ill-understood passages of Scripture, we know how they would be regarded by educated men. Would it be too much to call them fools? And if these masters employed force and persecution to secure the ascendancy of their insolent ignorance, would it be improper to speak of them as wild beasts?

The more the superstitions of the monks are despised, the more the bishops and priests are respected; while they do good, the monkish superstitions from Rome do nothing but evil. And of all these superstitions, is not the most dangerous that of hating one's neighbour on account of his opinions? And is it not evident that it would be even more reasonable to worship the sacred navel, the sacred prepuce, and the milk and dress of the Virgin Mary, than to detest and persecute one's brother?

VIRTUE BETTER THAN SCIENCE

The less we have of dogma, the less dispute; the less we have of dispute, the less misery. If that is not true, I am wrong.

Religion was instituted to make us happy in this world and the next. What must we do to be happy in the next world? Be just.[1] What must we do to be

---

[1] It may be useful to recall that, as earlier pages show, Voltaire did not believe in the " next world." Much of the phrasing of this part is, when it is not ironical, merely an *argumentum ad hominem.*—J. M.

happy in this world, as far as the misery of our nature allows?   Be indulgent.

It would be the height of folly to pretend to bring all men to have the same thoughts in metaphysics. It would be easier to subdue the whole universe by arms than to subdue all the minds in a single city.

Euclid easily persuaded all men of the truths of geometry.   How?   Because every single one of them is a corollary of the axiom, " Two and two make four." It is not exactly the same in the mixture of metaphysics and theology.

When Bishop Alexander and the priest Arius began [in the fourth century] to dispute as to the way in which the Logos emanated from the Father, the Emperor Constantine at first wrote to them as follows (as we find in Eusebius and Socrates) : " You are great fools to dispute about things you do not understand."

If the two parties had been wise enough to perceive that the emperor was right, the Christian world would not have been stained with blood for three hundred years.

What, indeed, can be more stupid and more horrible than to say to men : " My friends, it is not enough to be loyal subjects, submissive children, tender fathers, just neighbours, and to practise every virtue, cultivate friendship, avoid ingratitude, and worship Christ in peace; you must, in addition, know how one is engendered from all eternity, and how to distinguish the *homoousion* in the *hypostasis*, or we shall condemn you to be burned for ever, and will meantime put you to death " ?

Had such a proposition been made to Archimedes, or Poseidonius, or Varro, or Cato, or Cicero, what would he have said ?

Constantine did not persevere in his resolution to impose silence on the contending parties.   He might have invited the leaders of the pious frenzy to his palace and asked them what authority they had to disturb the world : " Have you the title-deeds of the divine family? What does it matter to you whether the Logos was made or engendered, provided men are loyal to him, preach a sound morality, and practise it as far as they can? I have done many wrong things in my time, and so have you. You are ambitious, so am I. The empire has cost me much knavery and cruelty; I have murdered nearly all my relatives. I repent, and would expiate my crimes by restoring peace to the Roman Empire. Do not prevent me from doing the only good that can efface my earlier barbarity. Help me to end my days in peace." Possibly he would have had no influence on the disputants; possibly he would have been flattered to find himself, in long red robe, his head covered with jewels, presiding at a council.

Yet this it was that opened the gate to all the plagues that came from Asia upon the West. From every disputed verse of Scripture there issued a fury armed with a sophism and a sword, that goaded men to madness and cruelty. The marauding Huns and Goths and Vandals did infinitely less harm; and the greatest harm they did was to join themselves in these fatal disputes.

OF UNIVERSAL TOLERATION

One does not need great art and skilful eloquence to prove that Christians ought to tolerate each other— nay, even to regard all men as brothers. Why, you say, is the Turk, the Chinese, or the Jew my brother? Assuredly; are we not all children of the same father, creatures of the same God?

But these people despise us and treat us as idolaters. Very well; I will tell them that they are quite wrong. It seems to me that I might astonish, at least, the stubborn pride of a Mohammedan or a Buddhist priest if I spoke to them somewhat as follows:—

This little globe, which is but a point, travels in space like many other globes; we are lost in the immensity. Man, about five feet high, is certainly a small thing in the universe. One of these imperceptible beings says to some of his neighbours, in Arabia or South Africa : " Listen to me, for the God of all these worlds has enlightened me. There are nine hundred million little ants like us on the earth, but my ant-hole alone is dear to God. All the others are eternally reprobated by him. Mine alone will be happy."

They would then interrupt me, and ask who was the fool that talked all this nonsense. I should be obliged to tell them that it was themselves. I would then try to appease them, which would be difficult.

I would next address myself to the Christians, and would venture to say to, for instance, a Dominican friar—an inquisitor of the faith : " Brother, you are aware that each province in Italy has its own dialect, and that people do not speak at Venice and Bergamo as they do at Florence. The Academy of La Crusca has fixed the language. Its dictionary is a rule that has to be followed, and the grammar of Matei is an infallible guide. But do you think that the consul of the Academy, or Matei in his absence, could in conscience cut out the tongues of all the Venetians and the Bergamese who persisted in speaking their own dialect ? "

The inquisitor replies : " The two cases are very different. In our case it is a question of your eternal salvation. It is for your good that the heads of the inquisition direct that you shall be seized on the information of any one person, however infamous or criminal; that you shall have no advocate to defend you; that the name of your accuser shall not be made known to you; that the inquisitor shall promise you pardon and then condemn you; and that you shall then be subjected to five kinds of torture, and afterwards either flogged or sent to the galleys or ceremoniously burned. On this Father Ivonet, Doctor Chucalon, Zanchinus, Campegius, Royas, Telinus, Gomarus, Diabarus, and Gemelinus are explicit, and this pious practice admits of no exception." [1]

I would take the liberty of replying: "Brother, possibly you are right. I am convinced that you wish to do me good. But could I not be saved without all that?"

It is true that these absurd horrors do not stain the face of the earth every day; but they have often done so, and the record of them would make up a volume much longer than the gospels which condemn them. Not only is it cruel to persecute, in this brief life, those who differ from us, but I am not sure if it is not too bold to declare that they are damned eternally. It seems to me that it is not the place of the atoms of a moment, such as we are, thus to anticipate the decrees of the Creator. Far be it from me to question the principle, "Out of the Church there is no salvation." I respect it, and all that it teaches; but do we really know all the ways of God, and the full range of his mercies? May we not hope in him as much as fear him? Is it not enough to be loyal to the Church? Must each individual usurp the rights of the Deity, and decide, before he does, the eternal lot of all men?

When we wear mourning for a king of Sweden, Denmark, England, or Prussia, do we say that we wear mourning for one who burns eternally in hell? There are in Europe forty million people who are not of the Church of Rome. Shall we say to each of them: "Sir, seeing that you are infallibly damned, I will neither eat, nor deal, nor speak with you"?

What ambassador of France, presented in audience to the Sultan, would say in the depths of his heart: "His Highness will undoubtedly burn for all eternity because he has been circumcised"? If he really believed that the Sultan is the mortal enemy of God, the object of his vengeance, could he speak to him? Ought he to be sent to him? With whom could we have intercourse? What duty of civil life could we

[1] See that excellent work, *The Manual of the Inquisition.*

ever fulfil if we were really convinced that we were dealing with damned souls?

Followers of a merciful God, if you were cruel of heart; if, in worshipping him whose whole law consisted in loving one's neighbour as oneself, you have burdened this pure and holy law with sophistry and unintelligible disputes; if you had lit the fires of discord for the sake of a new word or a single letter of the alphabet; if you had attached eternal torment to the omission of a few words or ceremonies that other peoples could not know, I should say to you :—

"Transport yourselves with me to the day on which all men will be judged, when God will deal with each according to his works. I see all the dead of former ages and of our own stand in his presence. Are you sure that our Creator and Father will say to the wise and virtuous Confucius, to the lawgiver Solon, to Pythagoras, to Zaleucus, to Socrates, to Plato, to the divine Antonines, to the good Trajan, to Titus, the delight of the human race, to Epictetus, and to so many other model men : ' Go, monsters, go and submit to a chastisement infinite in its intensity and duration; your torment shall be as eternal as I. And you, my beloved, Jean Chatel, Ravaillac, Damiens, Cartouche, etc. [assassins in the cause of the Church], who have died with the prescribed formulæ, come and share my empire and felicity for ever.' " [1]

You shrink with horror from such sentiments; and, now that they have escaped me, I have no more to say to you.

---

[1] This horrible doctrine must not wholly be relegated to the eighteenth century and the Middle Ages. It is still solemn Catholic doctrine, defined by the Vatican Council in 1870, that no atheist or agnostic, whether in good or bad faith, can be saved.—J. M.

GREAT BOOKS IN PHILOSOPHY PAPERBACK SERIES

ETHICS

SOCIAL AND POLITICAL PHILOSOPHY

GREAT MINDS PAPERBACK SERIES

ECONOMICS

RELIGION

SCIENCE

HISTORY

SOCIOLOGY

(Prices subject to change without notice.)